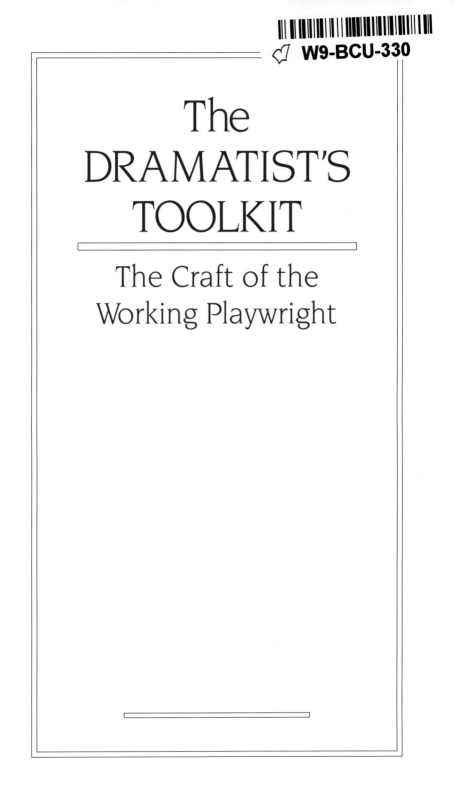

The
DRAMATIST'S
TOOLKIT

The Craft of the
Working Playwright

The DRAMATIST'S TOOLKIT

The Craft of the Working Playwright

Jeffrey Sweet

HEINEMANN
PORTSMOUTH, NEW HAMPSHIRE

HEINEMANN
A division of Reed Elsevier Inc.
361 Hanover Street
Portsmouth, NH 03801–3912
Offices and agents throughout the world

Editor: Lisa A. Barnett
Production: Renée M. Pinard
Text and cover design: Joni Doherty
Cover photo © 1993 by Trix Rosen

Excerpts from "The Award" and "Cover" by Jeffrey Sweet reprinted by
permission of the author. For performance rights, amateur or professional,
of "Cover" from *25 10-Minute Plays from Actors Theatre of Louisville*, please
contact Samuel French, Inc., 45 West 25th Street, New York, NY
10010–2751. Inquiries about Jeffrey Sweet's work—pieces excerpted in this
book or otherwise—may be directed to Susan Schulman Literary Agency,
454 West 44th Street, New York, NY   10036.

The author encourages correspondence. His internet numbers are
DGSWEET@aol.com or 73707.772@cis.com.

Library of Congress Cataloging-in-Publication Data
Sweet, Jeffrey, 1950–
    The dramatist's toolkit : the craft of the working playwright /
Jeffrey Sweet.
        p.   cm.
    ISBN 0–435–08629–4
    1. Playwriting.   2. Drama—Technique.   I. Title.
PN1661.S84   1993
808.2—dc20   93–14476
                                                                   CIP

Printed in the United States of America on acid-free paper
    99 98 97 96 95   BB   3 4 5 6 7 8 9

*For my father,
my first writing teacher*

CONTENTS

ACKNOWLEDGMENTS ix

INTRODUCTION xi

CHAPTER ONE
Where Playwrights Come From 1

CHAPTER TWO
Starting Principles 7

CHAPTER THREE
Negotiations 21

CHAPTER FOUR
Structure 29

CHAPTER FIVE
About Characters 39

CHAPTER SIX
Roles in Conflict 55

CHAPTER SEVEN
Exposition and Expectations 61

CHAPTER EIGHT
Dialogue 79

CHAPTER NINE
Violating Rituals 93

CHAPTER TEN
Musicals 99

CHAPTER ELEVEN
Screenwriting 109

CHAPTER TWELVE
The Right Space 115

CHAPTER THIRTEEN
The Literal and the Metaphoric 121

CHAPTER FOURTEEN
Ethics 125

CHAPTER FIFTEEN
Learning Experiences 139

CHAPTER SIXTEEN
Practical Advice 149

CHAPTER SEVENTEEN
Parting Words 159

ACKNOWLEDGMENTS

THIS BOOK STARTED WITH A LUNCH IN A VENTURA BOULEVARD deli when my friend (and later, collaborator) Melissa Manchester told me of her interest in writing for the stage and asked me to discuss some technical questions with her. This led me to write a series of letters on craft. At the suggestion of S. Ezra Goldstein, then the editor of *Dramatics*, a magazine published by the International Thespian Society, I polished versions of these letters into a series called "The Negotiating Stage" for that publication in 1983–84. Though little of the actual text of those letters appears here, writing and revising them required me to think in a disciplined way about a number of craft-related topics for the first time.

Most of the chapters in this book appeared, in different versions, as installments of "The Playwrights' Corner," the column for *Back Stage*, which its editor Sherry Eaker generously offered me in 1990. Michele LaRue, associate editor of *Back Stage*, has been very helpful in keeping me on track there. Earlier drafts of other chapters originally appeared as articles in *The Writer*, that fine and useful magazine edited by Sylvia K. Burack. Other material was first written for *The Dramatists Guild Quarterly*, with the encouragement of its longtime editor, Otis L. Guernsey, Jr. Clive Barnes, who was one of my professors at NYU, did me a great kindness by introducing me to Otis in the first place.

Many of the ideas herein originated as a result of conversations and workshops with alumni of Compass and Second City; I particularly want to thank Viola Spolin, Paul Sills, Del Close,

Sheldon Patinkin, Mike Nichols, Richard Schaal, Alan Arkin, and Bernard Sahlins for what I learned from them about improvisation. I do not claim that what follows represents their philosophies (I know that some of these people would disagree with much of what I propound), but I would not have arrived at some of these ideas had they not taken time with me. I also want to remember the late Lehman Engel who, in the Musical Theater Workshop sponsored by Broadcast Music, Inc., said much that was provocative and stimulating about writing musicals.

Much of this book also originated in response to questions from students at the various schools and institutions where I've had the pleasure to work, so nods are due to classes and workshop participants at Columbia University, the State University of New York at Purchase, Hofstra, the O'Neill Theater Center, HB Studios, New Dramatists, the Victory Gardens Theater, the Drama Project, the Atlanta New Plays Project, and the Chicago Dramatists Workshop. Thanks, too, to Maggie Grove and Jason Milligan, past and present directors of special projects at the Dramatists Guild, who offered me opportunities and forums to discuss craft with many of my fellow members.

I owe special gratitude to the members of the New York Writers' Bloc, who indulged my experiments and unselfishly shared their insights and enthusiasm over a period of years and oceans of coffee.

My father, James Sweet, was kind enough to lend this book his editorial eye. Among critical colleagues, Richard Christiansen, Julius Novick, and Dan Sullivan raised questions that prompted further thoughts, as did Sheldon Harnick.

And my deepest thanks to Lisa Barnett, my editor at Heinemann, for the questions, feedback, and enthusiasm that helped bring this long-contemplated project out of the realm of speculation to the point of being in your hands now.

INTRODUCTION

IF YOU'RE A DRAMATIST, YOU LIVE IN TWO WORLDS.

One is of your own creation. You set the scene, people it with characters, and establish the logic that dictates their behavior. Your dramatis personae struggle, prevail, or succumb according to your intentions. You call the tune. You set the rules.

The other world is the professional world. The world of directors, producers, actors, agents, and audience. You try to affect these people—to win their enthusiasm for your work—but only playwrights suffering from delusions would claim they are in charge. You can't set the rules here any more than you can negotiate with gravity. But you *can learn* the rules and use them to your advantage as you pursue productions.

To succeed as a working dramatist, you have to have skills in both of these worlds.

Though God knows it's difficult to write a fine play, doing so isn't enough. You have to know how to shepherd the play from page to stage. The theater, after all, requires collaboration with other people. Inevitably, this involves negotiating with what are frequently demanding colleagues. The consequently necessary political skills have little to do with purely creative talents.

But, of course, all the political skills in the world won't make poorly conceived or badly executed work hold the stage. You aren't likely to have the luxury of demanding colleagues if you haven't written something that makes them want to *be* colleagues in the first place.

This book is intended to address questions that arise in both worlds. In the earlier chapters, I deal with issues of pure craft, presenting theories on how plays are built. Later in the book, the emphasis shifts to professional issues—the challenges dramatists meet trying to get their plays produced and produced well.

A number of playwrights shy away from craft discussions with the same fear that primitive tribes of anecdote supposedly feel when faced with cameras they believe will steal their souls. For some, writing is a divine mystery, and they view the attempt to make concrete statements about how it is done as equivalent to trying to jam God into a glass jar like a firefly. Their method (if you can call something so amorphous a method) is to somehow open up channels of inspiration—pipelines to unchartable reservoirs of the intuitive. They are leery of tampering with what works for them, afraid that analysis will throw such a harsh light as to scare off skittish muses.

Which is not to say that some wonderful plays haven't been written by what I would call intuitive writers. I gather from what I've read that Tennessee Williams was one, and you don't get much better than A *Streetcar Named Desire*. But an intuitive writer does not offer much by way of concrete guidance. Anyone reading Tennessee Williams's *Memoirs* for a how-to in dramaturgy will be disappointed. You'll find more than you care to know (at any rate more than I cared to know) about his sex life, but the stuff that was truly intimate to him—about how he wrote some of the American theater's most enduring works—he kept as private as most of us keep *our* sex lives. I think it's because he didn't really *know* how he did it. He just did it, and when it felt good, the work that came out was brilliant. This noncraft approach doesn't make him any less of a writer, but it makes him a less than useful teacher, except by example.

In contrast, Stephen Sondheim, in addition to being the great composer-lyricist of our time, is a very conscious craftsman. He *does* know how he does it. What's more, as anyone who has had the pleasure of listening to him speak at length or who has read his articles in the The *Dramatists Guild Quarterly* knows, he has a talent for conveying these principles. This is not to say that sometimes he doesn't get the exhilarating sensation when the work seems to be writing itself. But he doesn't sit around waiting for inspiration to knock. He analyzes his problems and brings his considerable resources and tools to bear on solving them.

As you've probably gathered, I prefer the Sondheim approach. To me, trying to write by relying totally on inspiration is analogous to a surgeon trying to perform an operation by relying on occasional flashes of lightning. I want the lights on. I want to see the tools—the scalpel, the clamps, and so forth.

Besides, a scene you initially approach as a technical challenge may soon start coming more organically. It's rather like dealing with a car that refuses to start. Sometimes when the battery is weak, giving the car a push and popping the clutch will get the motor going. For me, technique serves a similar function to the push and pop—it builds sufficient momentum to engage the motor of the play.

Most of the examples I use are drawn from well-known plays, though I also refer to films and television series. There are indisputable technical differences between writing for these media and writing for the theater (some of which I discuss), but what the tasks have in common outweighs how they differ. Whether in stage play, screenplay, or teleplay, the challenge, after all, is to tell stories through actors. Most of the techniques I discuss in these pages apply to all forms of dramatic writing.

The purpose of technique is to help overcome the internal obstacles to realizing your work. But, as I mentioned above, there are a lot of external considerations. Despite the fact that so much of the dramatist's work is done alone, there are aspects of this profession that require interaction with the so-called outside world. In the second section of this book, I explore some of these aspects: the nonprofit managements who are most likely to launch new work, the Dramatists Guild, suggestions for the organization of writers' workshops, as well as some of the questions you must consider if you are offered a production.

The students in my workshops and many of the writers I've worked with in various supervisory capacities seem to have found the techniques I describe here of concrete value in facing their dramatic problems, and I hope you will, too. I don't pretend that this book covers everything that can possibly be said about craft, but it is a fairly comprehensive expression of my ideas on the technical aspects of dramatic writing. (At least for now. The more I teach, the more questions I'm asked, the more thinking is required to deal with the questions. Much of what is enclosed here began with students pressing me on various points, and I'm grateful for their persistence.)

Some of what is in this book is what I think is demonstrably valid, statements that may be measured against observable reality.

And some is hard-core opinion with which you may violently disagree.

To which I say—fine. Think through your objections. Build on them. In your response you will find the seeds of your own philosophy of dramatic writing.

Where Playwrights Come From

AFTER YEARS OF TEACHING DRAMATIC TECHNIQUE, I HAVE strong ideas about what kinds of people are most likely to become real, working playwrights: actors and journalists. Not novelists.

This may sound odd, given that both novelists and playwrights compose works featuring characters, plots, themes, and so forth. But the difference in the manners in which they tell their stories is crucial.

The novel is a form of literature. Literature is writing that offers a full and satisfying experience when read. Most plays—even some of the best—do not offer such a reading experience. So, the playscript is by definition not a literary form.

Please don't misunderstand me. I'm not saying that there aren't scripts that transcend their form by being "good reads." Obviously most of Shakespeare reads very nicely. But the ultimate test of a script is not how well it reads but how well it *plays*, and there is no necessary correlation between the two.

Take, for instance, Chekhov. Now, I happen to be a great Chekhov enthusiast, but I find his plays unsatisfying when encountered on the page. To give you an example of what I mean: In the fourth act of *The Cherry Orchard*, Lopakhin states his intention to stop shilly-shallying and finally propose marriage to Varya, something she and everybody else in the play have been expecting him to do for a long time. No sooner has he announced this intention than Varya enters, claiming to be searching for something. Lopakhin and Varya are alone. They talk a little—a very little—ending with a word or two about the weather. Then Lopakhin exits.

That's about it. That's what is in black and white on the page. Some awkward small talk and an exit. When I first read it, the scene didn't make much of an impression on me.

When I finally saw it on stage, however, I was literally brought to tears. Underneath the small talk, the scene is about repression and the death of hope. Mind you, neither Lopakhin nor Varya talks about repression and the death of hope. It is embodied not in what they say, but in what they do and in what we understand their actions to mean. Unfortunately for the reader, little of what they do and virtually none of what it means are explicit on the page. These values only emerge clearly in performance, which is all right because, having been written for the stage, that is where the values are supposed to emerge.

So here we have a script that is an unsatisfying reading experience (for me, at any rate) and is thus, by the criterion I offered above, not effective literature.

Nonetheless, it is a masterpiece. If its greatness doesn't reside in the quality of its language, then it must reside in the quality of the behavior the actors are challenged to create to give life to the text.

So, if a script isn't literature, what is it?

It is a program of opportunities for actors to do things designed to rivet the attention and sympathies of the audience. Sometimes, yes, among the things the actors do is speak. I'd be the last to deny the importance of language in the theater. But there is a lot more to a play than a bunch of people saying words. Indeed, the words have meaning only within the context of the players' actions.

Sophisticated actors understand that the quality of a part is not to be determined by counting the number of lines it contains or the quality of the language. Some great parts have either no lines or very few: the daughter in Bertolt Brecht's Mother Courage, for one. She is a mute, so, of course, Brecht has written no speeches for her. But who can forget the scene in which she rings a bell in order to warn a sleeping town it is about to be attacked, even though she knows it to be an act of virtual suicide? Not a word of dialogue, but one hell of a part.

And what about Helen Keller in William Gibson's *The Miracle Worker*? The only words she's assigned are, "Wah-wah, wah-wah." Not exactly a daunting memorization task. But, of course, there's much more to the role. Before she gets to the water pump and makes the thrilling connection between what is coming out of it and the collection of symbols that represent it, we've had a couple of hours of her highly theatrical confrontations with teacher Annie Sullivan. Even without many lines, the part is a platform for virtuoso work, as a look at the awards on Patty Duke's mantle would attest.

It is this concept—this business of the actor's job primarily being to act rather than speak (which is why the job is named "actor" rather than "speaker")—that novelists tend not to understand. And it is for lack of this understanding they commonly come to grief when they attempt to write for the stage. Go down the roll call of celebrated American novelists. Many of them have tried to write plays. Few of them have succeeded in writing workable stage pieces. When is the last time you saw a stirring production of Ernest Hemingway's *The Fifth Column*? How about William Faulkner's *Requiem for a Nun*? Saul Bellow, Joseph Heller, John Updike, Mark Twain, Bret Harte, Norman Mailer, E. L. Doctorow, and Henry James all took shots at the theater at one time or another. Nobody would claim that their scripts are to be numbered among their enduring works. Yes, I know, John Steinbeck's name is on the stage version of *Of Mice and Men*, but it is commonly accepted that the production's director, George S. Kaufman, had a large hand in the adaptation. (Some novelists have been credited with decent screenplays, but the politics of screenwriting make it difficult to determine how much credit belongs to those novelists. Writers frequently write their scripts in close consultation with directors, so novelists' inclination to wordiness may be neutralized by their more powerful collaborators. Howard Hawkes may very well have curtailed William Faulkner's habitual verbosity in their very free adaptation of Ernest Hemingway's *To Have and Have*

Not. Also, many scripts are the product of a variety of hands that may go uncredited. I've done a fair amount of uncredited script doctoring myself. I once did a top-to-bottom rewrite of a TV movie as a "creative consultant," only to see the writer who had quit the project be nominated for an Emmy for my script. Ah, Hollywood.)

What is the reason for novelists' bad track record in the theater? Literary artists are accustomed to thinking of the word as the basic unit of their art. They use combinations of words to generate images and trains of thought in the reader's mind. When they attempt scripts, they tend to carry over their habit of trying to accomplish everything with language. The result is usually a lot of talk—big chunks of undiluted speechifying in which characters articulate the Themes.

True stage artists, however, know that the basic unit of the theater is not the word but the actor.

After all, when you come right down to it, the only two elements you *have* to have to make theater are actors and audience. In fact, the genealogy of all of the other theatrical disciplines may be traced back to these two essential and irreducible functions. The first set designer may have been an actor who decided to do his or her tiger imitation in front of the waterfall. The first director may have been a friend who said, "No, make the growl *louder*. *Feel* it!" The first playwright may have been a player who planned the routine ahead of time. (And the first critic may have been the soul sitting in the audience who threw a rotten papaya stageward in the middle of a show.)

Logically, then, playwriting is an extension of acting. Once upon a time, in preliterate cultures, actors made up their own material. (You can get a whiff of this tradition at improvisational theaters such as Second City, where material is generated spontaneously in front of an audience and then pulled into rehearsal to be polished into finished pieces by the company.) As time went on and specialization set in, actors, by and large, found their prerogatives narrowed to interpreting material generated by others.

Many of these others, in fact, began as actors or had some experience performing. Shakespeare and Molière, of course, wrote parts for themselves, and there are accounts of Greek masters taking part in performances of their works. Among dramatists from this century, the list of well-known playwrights with acting in their backgrounds includes Harold Pinter, David Mamet, Betty Comden, Adolph Green, Alan Bennett, George Abbott, Noel Coward, Alan Ayckbourn, Beth Henley, Christopher Durang, Charles Gordone, Jason Miller, Craig Lucas, and Frank Galati. Having faced the task of creating life from the hints in other writers' texts, such writers have a strong sense of what's playable, which in turn informs their own texts. They can spot where people cast in their scripts are likely to run into trouble. By the same token, they can draw on memories of scenes they played that worked and extrapolate from them principles for creating effective scenes of their own.

Why do I name journalists along with actors as offering particular promise as playwrights? The good reporter has developed a strong sense of where the event is. In a straight news context—as opposed to the editorial page—he or she is trained to present the necessary and relevant information without overt comment and to do so succinctly and concretely. All of these skills are directly applicable to playwriting.

In fact, there once was no distinction between actors and journalists. To return to the preliterate world, in a tribal society the actor *was* a journalist. For instance, when American Indians went on a hunt or a battle, they knew that they would be expected to give a report to the folks back home covering the deeds of their expedition. It wasn't a matter of bragging; it was a matter of their fellow tribe members having the right to know what was done in their name. So, on the trip back to the village, the braves would, well, perhaps "rehearse" is not quite the word, but they would discuss how to present their news at the big meeting that marked their return. That presentation surely must be counted as both a journalistic and theatrical event.

The reportorial tradition is most apparent today in the work of such artists as Spalding Gray, Eric Bogosian, Lily Tomlin,

Anna Deavere Smith, and (when she's doing solo work) Whoopi Goldberg, who bear witness by transforming their observations and experiences into a kind of theatrical testimony.

Perhaps the list of successful playwrights who started as journalists is not as long as the list of those who began as actors, but still, there are some pretty significant talents who did time describing to their papers' readership the facts of the world they covered—Ben Hecht and Charles MacArthur (naturally), William Inge, Marsha Norman, Richard Nelson, and Charles L. Mee, Jr.

I don't mean to discourage those of you who write prose fiction from taking the plunge. I only mean to caution that you should be prepared for an apprenticeship learning new principles and skills because the old ones don't necessarily apply.

I don't think these new principles and skills are all that difficult to assimilate if properly explained. And, in the next chapter, I start trying to do just that.

2

CHAPTER

Starting Principles

YOU'RE A BEGINNING MUSIC STUDENT. YOU ARRIVE AT YOUR FIRST class, and the teacher launches into a sophisticated discussion of the sonata form and the use of inversion in thematic development and God knows what else. At the end of the session comes the first homework assignment: bring in preliminary sketches for a symphony.

I imagine your reaction would be something like, "Sketches for a *symphony*?! Give me a break! I don't know how to read *music* yet!"

And you would be right. It is nonsense to attempt to structure a large-scale musical work if you haven't yet learned the basics of notation, much less the principles of harmony, counterpoint, and orchestration.

But many of the books that purport to teach playwriting do something similar: They begin by sailing into exegeses on structure without dealing with the dramatic equivalents of notation, harmony, counterpoint, and orchestration. In the process, I think they do a good deal of harm by encouraging people to begin work on plays prematurely.

I find little more frustrating than to encounter a play with an exciting premise that has been botched because the playwright hadn't acquired the technique to realize its promise. Nobody would dream of giving a beginning sculptor a huge hunk of rare marble with which to attempt his or her first piece. Nobody would be so foolish as to hand over to an apprentice chef an expensive wine to play with in making his or her maiden effort in haute cuisine. But many of the "how-to" writing books commonly advise the inexperienced playwright to begin by try-ing to plot out that great idea for a play he or she has been mulling over for years, disregarding the fact that the inexperi-enced playwright by definition doesn't yet have what musicians call "the chops" to do it justice. And so some very good ideas are turned into unsuccessful plays.

You shouldn't begin writing a play if you haven't mastered the craft of writing a scene. And you can't write a scene without knowing something about how actors work and what the play-wright has to supply so that they can do that work.

In order to play a scene, an actor has to know a few things about the character. Some of these things are what I call the concrete aspects: the character's physical condition, sexual orientation, education, nationality, and so forth. If an actor is cast as Quasimodo in a dramatization of *The Hunchback of Notre Dame*, for instance, he knows he's going to be creating a person who is extremely deformed, deaf (from the bells), heterosexual, uneducated, and French. Any other acting choices he makes must be consistent with these givens.

In addition to these concrete aspects, the actor has to know what the character wants, which brings us to that much-bandied term, the "objective." Everything the character does is in some way in pursuit of the character's overarching objective, the big thing that he or she wants and will go to extremes to achieve. In fact, it is these extremes that make a character memorable.

This ties in with what I wrote earlier, that the actor's job is to create compelling behavior. Now, *all* behavior—small or large—is motivated. If I do something as trivial as scratch my back, it is motivated by the desire to relieve the irritation of an itch. If Medea butchers her children, it is to impress upon Jason how angry she is about him ditching her.

So, the actor looks at the script to glean what the character's major objective is and, under the guidance of the director, makes choices in the creation of behavior that supports the pursuit of this objective and is consistent with the text.

It is very important to understand, though, that what the characters want is not necessarily (1) what they *say* they want, or (2) what they consciously *think* they want. Sometimes characters pursue objectives that exist on a subconscious plane, ones that they might even consciously disavow. Under such circumstances, actors must know more than the characters they play. For instance, Eddie Carbone in Arthur Miller's A *View from the Bridge* never *says* anything about being carnally attracted to his niece. Nor do I believe Eddie consciously acknowledges this attraction until the end of the play. Yet this attraction is very much at the root of how he behaves, and the actor playing Eddie has to assimilate this in order to create behavior that fulfills Miller's intentions.

Part of the skill of acting resides in creating the illusion of *not* knowing more than the character, to be so thoroughly under the character's skin—to so completely inhabit the character's soul—as to give the audience no tip-off that there is any difference between the actor and the character. Actors without this skill to submerge themselves in the parts they play run the risk of indicating—commenting on their roles. The actor who plays a villain by twirling a mustache and chuckling malevolently is indicating. So is the actress whose approach to the role of an ingenue includes poking at a dimple with her forefinger and fluttering her eyes in an attempt to convey innocence. Both actors in these (admittedly) exaggerated examples are trying to communicate directly to the audience how they want their characters to be viewed, as opposed to simply playing the characters truthfully and leaving the job of evaluating to the audience. In so doing, such actors draw the audience's attention to their *performance* rather than fostering belief in the characters they are playing. To tell an actor that he or she indicates is on a par with telling a singer that he or she is constantly off-key. Indicating is the big taboo of naturalistic acting.

In the previous chapter, I wrote that playwriting is an extension of acting. I believe, too, that faulty technique in playwriting is often a corollary of faulty technique in acting. Actors are not the only ones liable to indicate. Dramatists, too, may succumb to the temptation of commenting on or evaluating their work in their texts. Usually this manifests itself in the script's most ornately written, showpiece speeches—the ones in which it is apparent that the writer is particularly impressed by his or her own eloquence, often at the expense of the characters' credibility. The passages that writers most admire in their own work are the ones in which they are most likely to have slipped into preaching or not-so-veiled self-congratulation.

This point brings me back to A *View from the Bridge*. I think it contains much of Arthur Miller's most exciting work, partially because most of the characters, not being well-educated and verbally adroit, often communicate in large, highly charged gestures. Think of Eddie trying to impugn Rodolpho's masculinity by kissing him on the mouth. Think, too, of Eddie and Marco having a contest of strength by seeing who can pick up a chair by the end of one leg. These are powerful scenes, ones in which the relationships between the characters are made vivid through action.

There's only one serious problem in the play. His name is Alfieri. He is the lawyer who acts as narrator. He comes on at the beginning of the play to tell us, essentially, that although this story takes place on the docks and the people don't speak English so good . . . we're talking classical themes here. Another lawyer, says Alfieri, ''in some Caesar's year'' may well have ''heard the same complaint and sat there powerless as I, and watched it run its bloody course.'' In so writing, Miller stops about three inches short of turning on a neon sign announcing, ''This is a Tragedy.'' Instead of allowing the audience to evaluate the play for themselves, through his alter ago Miller announces his own opinion of the significance of the work to follow. This is equivalent to the stand-up comic who begins by saying, ''I'm funny and I'm going to make you laugh.''

These kinds of evaluations are properly the province of the audience. Our job as writers is to put dramatic action on the stage; then we should get the hell out of the way and trust the members of the audience to discern its significance for themselves. In short, the premises belong onstage, the conclusions belong in the house.

If you've had a brush with the study of logic, you probably remember that premises and conclusions are components of something called a syllogism. A simple syllogism consists of two premises (or pieces of information) followed by a conclusion (a statement of a new understanding derived from the premises).

Premise one: All Martians love Debussy. Premise two: Reginald is a Martian. Conclusion: Reginald loves Debussy.

What has this to do with theater? Quite a lot.

Our goal as playwrights is to engage the audience in our characters and their dilemmas. The way to get an audience engaged is to stimulate them to fill in for themselves what is left unsaid.

If I write the equation $2+3=5$ and show it to you, you'll probably shrug and nod your bored acknowledgment that it's true, a fairly passive response. If, on the other hand, I write $2+x=5$, your immediate impulse will be to fill in that x. This reaction is not passive but active. You are *involved* in the equation, almost involuntarily.

Similarly, to keep our audiences involved in our stories, I believe we dramatists should offer the theatrical equivalent of x's to fill in. The little math problem I just gave you is analogous to the syllogism without the conclusion. (In fact, logic is a branch of mathematics.)

So, in order to engage the people in the audience, you present just enough information (premises) for them to figure out for themselves the meaning of what's going on onstage (the conclusions).

How?

For a revue called *Holding Patterns*, I wrote a sketch called "The Award." Lerner, a well-dressed man in his thirties, has just been given an award at a public function in his honor. Clutching his plaque, he addresses the audience to express his gratitude.

LERNER. Thank you. This is an honor I never dreamed I'd—I mean, the Charles Jensen Briggs Award! There are so many people to thank. Professor Herman Krause, who was the first to encourage me. The Leona Fielding Foundation for the funding, because, let's face it, this does cost money. And, of course, my colleagues in the lab—Ira Crutcher, Fred Jory, Anita Pleshowsky and Andy Kramer. And of course, I want to—Wait a second, did I say Anita

Pleshowsky? I'm sorry. I meant Anita Petrakoff. Petrakoff, Pleshowsky—you can see how I might, uh, confuse— (*Trying to remember.*) Pleshowsky. Anita Pleshowsky—Oh, yes. I remember Anita Pleshow— . . . We were in junior high school together. That's right. Mr. Champion's homeroom. Oh yes, I used to think that Anita was about the neatest person in the world. I would write her notes in social studies. Also in music, English, math and hygiene. I would have written her notes in gym, but, of course, boys and girls don't do gym together. Though sometimes I would see her and the other girls in Mr. Champion's class running laps around the playground in their blue shorts and tops.

My feelings for Anita Pleshowsky were—Well, I thought about her, I dreamed about her, I followed her home and peeked through the window of Alma Kimball's school for charm where she took classes every Saturday at 10:30. She played very hard-to-get. If she saw me looking at her, she would look away, or make a face, or stick her tongue out.

And then, one day, Mr. Newman, the school counselor, called me into his office. He said to me, "Morris, um, I realize that you are a young man—a growing young person—and young people your age start to develop. And this development is sometimes awkward, sometimes painful. Sometimes we find ourselves attracted to another young person—a young lady, say—and we try to express our feelings. This is normal, this is natural. But sometimes the young lady in question doesn't feel the same way we do. This is something we must learn to accept. You in particular must learn to accept this because you find yourself in this situation. You know the young lady I'm referring to, Morris. Now, I think it would be best for everyone concerned if you cool it, OK? Do you understand what I mean? Good. You may go back to your class."

I think of this now. I think of Mr. Newman and the red wisps of hair on his knuckles. I think of the blush that I could feel suffusing my young cheeks upon learning that my secret yearnings and communications were not as secret as I had hoped. I think of these things, and I laugh.

For I have gotten over you, Anita Pleshowsky. You were once the object of my fantasies and daydreams, but that was fifteen years ago, and a lot of time has passed. Other women—nicer than you, smarter than you, prettier than you—have favored me with their company, and not one of them ever found cause to stick her tongue out at me.

I am beyond the reach of your cruelty. No, your sadism! I am untouched by it. Unmoved. If you were to phone me now, if you were to dial the number here—area code 212–555–3076—if you were to call and say, "Morris, I am sorry. Morris, I want you. Morris can you ever forgive me? Morris, please hold me in your arms and let me know the joy of you!"—I would hang up. Just try it and see.

   That number again is 212–555–3076.

   Thank you for this lovely award.

In this piece, what Lerner is literally saying is that he has gotten past the injury he felt from an unrequited teenage infatuation. But the audience weighs his assertion against the fact that he is relating a humiliation from fifteen years past during an awards ceremony attended by people to whom it cannot possibly have any serious meaning. What's more, he shifts from telling the story to the people attending the ceremony to addressing Anita Pleshowsky directly, challenging her to phone him if she doesn't believe that he has gotten over her.

So, though he insists he's gotten over her, the audience, evaluating his behavior, believes differently. His words and actions are the *premises* presented onstage. The *conclusion* in the audience is that, despite the passing of decades and his putative status as a grown up, Lerner continues to be obsessed with Anita Pleshowsky to such a degree as to revert to teenage behavior.

I said earlier that in analyzing a part, the actor examines the script to determine his or her character's objective. The actor, of necessity, is most concerned with an individual character's perspective.

By definition, the playwright's perspective is broader. In a simple, two-person scene, the playwright is dealing with two sets of objectives confronting each other. Character A wants something out of Character B, and Character B wants something out of Character A. The scene consists of the way they behave in the pursuit of their objectives.

I like to think of this as a negotiation. Where there is no negotiation, there is no scene.

Now, sometimes people do come straight out and articulate their objectives. "I want you to love me, Dad." But mostly they don't. Mostly people are not so explicit and direct about the basic issues in their lives. Frequently they aren't entirely *conscious* of the nature of these basic issues. (A lot of psychologists make good livings out of helping you become conscious on the optimistic assumption that, if you are, you will be empowered to make choices about what actions to take. They don't call shrinks ''analysts'' for nothing.) In such cases, instead of negotiating directly for what they want, people negotiate indirectly.

Perhaps you remember this experiment from a grade school science class: You place a sheet of paper over a magnet, then you pour iron filings onto the paper. Almost instantly, the filings arrange themselves into a pattern. The pattern indicates the outline of the magnetic field. You don't *see* the field itself. You see the *pattern* the filings make because of the presence of the field.

Similarly, any characters confronting one another onstage generate the emotional equivalent of a magnetic field. A well-chosen object placed between the characters will be affected by this emotional field in the same way that the filings are affected by the magnetic field. Just as you see the pattern of the magnetic field through the way it acts on the filings, you can get some sense of the nature of the emotional field through its impact on the object in question.

For example, Carol and Eddie are at the beginning of a relationship. One morning, after spending the night at his place, Carol emerges from the bathroom wearing his softball league T-shirt.

EDDIE. That's my T-shirt.
CAROL. Yes.
EDDIE. You're wearing my T-shirt.
CAROL. Fits pretty well, don't you think?
EDDIE. Well, yes, but—
CAROL. But what?
EDDIE. Well, it's *my* T-shirt.
CAROL. Unh-hunh? So?
EDDIE. My T-shirt that was in *my* drawer.
CAROL. Right. I took it out.
EDDIE. My point exactly.
CAROL. I'm sorry, I don't see what—
EDDIE. Never mind.

CAROL. No, obviously something is on your mind, or you wouldn't
have brought it up.

EDDIE. It's OK. Forget it.

CAROL. No, if this is going to work between us, we have to be open
with each other. We have to share our feelings.

EDDIE. All right. My feelings about the T-shirt are it's my T-shirt and
I wish you'd—you know—asked?

CAROL. Before putting it on?

EDDIE. Before taking it out of the drawer and putting it on. For that
matter, before opening the drawer.

CAROL. Asked to open the drawer?

EDDIE. Yes.

CAROL. Your permission?

EDDIE. "Permission" isn't quite how I'd put it—

CAROL. Would you want that in writing?

EDDIE. Never mind.

CAROL. If I'd known you'd get so upset—

EDDIE. I'm not upset.

CAROL. It's just a T-shirt.

EDDIE. That's right. That's all it is. And I'm not upset. So let's just—
You want to go out for brunch or what?

Does anybody need a diagram to figure out what's going on
here?

The negotiation over the T-shirt provides the audience with
the premises. The audience responds by coming to conclusions
regarding the real issues underneath the wrangling.

A good way to ruin the scene would be to shove words like
territoriality and *fear of commitment* into it. They're unnecessary.
The audience is already there and feeling rather self- congratu-
latory about having arrived there without being nudged. For the
playwright to erect a neon sign saying, "This scene is about a
guy overreacting to a woman taking his 'space' for granted,"
would be insulting, Mickey Mousing, *indicating*.

It is because I think Miller is indicating with Alfieri that I
object to the passages I cited in A *View from the Bridge*. Putting a
character onstage who overtly states the themes of the script,
or otherwise interprets it for the audience, conveys the impression that the writer doesn't trust the audience to understand
the material without help. By pushing Alfieri downstage to tell
us, in effect, "Listen up, this is important and this is why,"

Miller is signaling that he doesn't have faith in our unaided powers of analysis. Whether he so intended, Miller is condescending to us by doing this. In playwriting, as in life, you're not likely to win good will with a condescending manner.

Part of the skill involved in using the technique of dramatizing the emotional field between characters through their negotiation over an object lies in the adroit *choice* of objects. Many of the great dramatists had a flair for heightening the effect of their scenes by choosing unusual or particularly dramatic objects.

The Elizabethan theaters had fewer technical resources than those to which we've grown accustomed. Shakespeare didn't have sophisticated machinery to move scenery on and off his stage. His lighting was whatever the sun afforded on a given day. Since his companies had several plays in repertory, the costuming was probably fairly generic, applicable to a variety of tales. So Shakespeare used special ingenuity in the objects he incorporated into his work. In fact, according to chroniclers of the time, it was with a scene containing a particularly impressive use of props that he first established his reputation as a "hot young playwright."

In Act I, scene 4 of *Henry* VI, *Part Three*, the Duke of York, who, with his sons, has led a revolt against Henry VI, has been captured by Margaret, Henry VI's bloodthirsty queen. Margaret steps forward to taunt York. She shows him a handkerchief with a red stain on it, and informs him in a casual way that it was dipped in the blood of his youngest and much-beloved son Rutland whom one of her followers has just killed. "And if thine eyes can water for his death," she says, "I give thee this to dry thy cheeks withal," and does indeed offer it to him. (In one particularly effective production I saw, York refused to take the handkerchief so she draped it over his shoulder.) Continuing with her cruel sport, Margaret goes on to say, in essence, "So you want to be a king, hunh? Well, let's see how you'd look in a crown." And she makes a paper crown, places it onto his head, and remarks sarcastically, "Ay, marry, sir, now looks he like a king!"

Powerful stuff, the power of which derives largely from the *physicalization* of York's downfall and Margaret's sadism by the introduction of two imaginatively chosen objects. The paper crown is a wonderful choice. Being paper, of course, it doesn't have the value of a real crown, which is an adroit way of conveying the contempt with which Margaret views York's aspirations for the throne. And the handkerchief, which she mockingly offers to comfort York in his grief, is drenched with fresh cause for that grief.

Shakespeare shows a flair for the adroit choice of objects throughout his plays. To mention certain props is to summon up vivid images of some of his most compelling scenes. Remember the use of the crown and the mirror in the abdication scene (Act IV, scene 1) of *Richard* II? Remember the handkerchief (another handkerchief!) in *Othello* and the three caskets from which Portia's suitors must choose in *The Merchant of Venice*, the ring in *Twelfth Night*, the leek in *Henry* V, and so on?

In fact, the famous scene in which the houses of Lancaster and York choose different colored roses (in Act II, scene 4 of *Henry* VI, *Part One*) has no basis in fact. As Isaac Asimov wrote in his invaluable *Asimov's Guide to Shakespeare*, the Yorks adopted the White Rose as their emblem sometime during the middle of the civil war, and it was only *after* the end of that war that those who sided against the White Rose of the Yorks chose the Red Rose as a symbol of their opposition. Certainly, during the fighting nobody referred to the conflict between the Yorks and Lancasters as the War of the Roses. But Shakespeare wasn't one to let the petty facts of history get in the way of effective drama, so he constructed a compelling scene in which the choice of colors visually underscores the choice of sides. (In the contest between art and the facts, art, being more vivid, usually prevails.)

Many modern playwrights have also demonstrated their resourcefulness through their choice of objects. Much of the action in Lillian Hellman's *The Little Foxes* revolves around a safe deposit box and the bonds stolen from it. In Frederick Knott's *Wait Until Dark*, the villains' actions are motivated by the desire to get their hands on a doll stuffed with drugs. In William Gibson's *The Miracle Worker*, Annie Sullivan and Helen Keller go head to head over a variety of objects—a key, a plate of food, a pile of silverware, and so on. The focal point of Donald Margulies's *Sight Unseen* is a nude a famous artist painted of his then-girlfriend when they were young, which he wishes to borrow from her (which, cleverly, Margulies never lets us see). And the third act of Ben Hecht and Charles MacArthur's *The Front Page* revolves around a rolltop desk in which two rough-and-tumble journalists have hidden an escaped murderer.

Act I, scene 2 of Tennessee Williams's A *Streetcar Named Desire* offers a virtuoso demonstration of the use of objects. As the first extended scene between Blanche and Stanley, it is composed of a series of confrontations over props and costumes. Among them are the red satin robe she wears as she emerges from the bathroom, the flowered print dress she changes into and the curtain she draws while she changes, the cigarette he smokes that she tries to get him to share, the buttons she asks him to help her with, and the clothes and jewelry he's pawed while rifling through her trunk. I don't know if the following bit of business originated with Williams or was discovered in rehearsal under Elia Kazan's direction of the original production, but it is a particularly telling moment: "She sprays herself with her atomizer; then playfully sprays him with it. He seizes the atomizer and slams it down on the dresser." And, of course, the scene's most charged objects—her late husband's love letters tied up in a ribbon. When Stanley "rips off the ribbon" to examine them, Blanche "snatches them from him," saying, "Now that you've touched them I'll burn them!" Between the negotiations over the atomizer, the letters, and the rest of the inventory, we get very strong evidence of Blanche's and Stanley's contrasting values and the irreconcilability between them that culminates in her destruction at his hands.

The *transformation* or *destruction* of an object introduced onstage can give a scene even greater impact. At the beginning of the third act of *The Odd Couple*, Neil Simon has Felix emerge from the kitchen with a plate of pasta. Furious at him, Oscar picks up an aerosol (an object associated with the finicky Felix) and sprays Felix's food. Then he orders Felix to get the spaghetti off the poker table. Felix laughs and tells Oscar it's not spaghetti, it's linguine. Oscar picks up the plate and hurls it (offstage) into the kitchen, crying, "Now it's garbage!" Felix refuses to clean it up. Oscar says he doesn't want it cleaned up. Felix makes a move to clean it up, and Oscar threatens injury if Felix so much as touches it. Though the action revolves around pasta, the real subject of the scene is not the disposition of the linguine but the deterioration of their relationship. The transformation of the food to garbage graphically dramatizes the disintegration of Felix and Oscar's relationship.

To return to Tennessee Williams, in *The Glass Menagerie*, the shy Laura shows Jim, the gentleman caller, her favorite piece from a collection of glass figures, a unicorn. In an effort to raise her spirits, Jim begins to waltz with Laura, but, during the dance, they bump into the table on which the unicorn is sitting. It falls to the floor and its horn breaks off. Later, when she realizes that Jim's visit will not be the beginning of the relationship between them for which she had hoped (during the scene, he reveals he has recently become engaged), Laura gives him the damaged unicorn as a souvenir. The shattering of the unicorn gives special emphasis to a scene concerned with the shattering of Laura's illusions.

Yes, the negotiation over objects is a technical device. But it's no artificial trick. One of the reasons this device works so well onstage is that it reflects the way people behave in real life, for we are constantly negotiating with each other. When a couple battles over the remote control to their TV set, through the arguments they advance in support of their respective choices, they're revealing their differing tastes. When children fight over who's going to sleep in the upper bunk, the resolution of their controversy tells a great deal about which child has what powers and prerogatives. And who hasn't been party to the problem of apportioning responsibility for a check in a restaurant?

To bring such negotiations to the stage is to reveal how, in contests over whatever is at hand, human beings often inadvertently reveal the deeper issues that lie between them.

3

CHAPTER

Negotiations

IN CHAPTER 2, I INTRODUCED THE IDEA OF VIEWING A SCENE AS A negotiation. Let's pursue this concept further.

In the simple form of a two-character encounter, A wants something out of B, and B wants something out of A. The meat of the scene has to do with the way the characters pursue what they want. There are essentially three possibilities as to the course this negotiation will take.

Sometimes, both parties will get what they want. In Act I, scene 4 of Joseph Stein's book for *Fiddler on the Roof*, Tevye and the butcher Lazar Wolf have a comic negotiation in which Tevye thinks Lazar Wolf is trying to purchase his milk cow, when in fact we in the audience know that he is asking for Tevye's daughter's hand in marriage. Once the confusion is cleared up, the two strike a bargain and sing "To Life." Such a scene is about identifying and removing the obstacles to agreement.

Sometimes one party will prevail over the other. In Act I, scene 2 of Shakespeare's *Richard* III, Richard overwhelms Anne, swiftly and audaciously transforming the widow of a man he killed from a curse-spewing enemy to a fiancee. Such a scene is about how one character seizes and holds the advantage.

And sometimes neither party will clearly prevail, resulting in a stalemate that leads to other negotiations later in the play. Certainly, in the first scenes between Blanche and Stanley in *Streetcar*, neither Blanche nor Stanley emerges the clear winner. Blanche wants Stanley to give her the kind of deference she thinks she's due; Stanley refuses to play along. Stanley wants Blanche to come down off her high horse and concede his higher claim to Stella's affections; Blanche tones down the twittering some, but she gives no real ground. Matters between them being unresolved, the contest clearly must continue, which, in a series of negotiations with increasingly heightened stakes, it does until the end of the play.

Whether or not one character is successful, the character who pursues his or her goal with the greater energy sets the agenda of the scene. In Act I, scene 1 of David Mamet's *Glengarry Glen Ross*, a struggling real estate salesman named Shelley Levene wants Williamson, the office manager, to give him better-quality leads so that he can have an improved shot at making sales and thus keep from being fired. Levene is willing to bribe Williamson for the leads. Williamson is willing to be bribed. But Williamson wants to be paid in advance, and Levene doesn't have the necessary cash on hand. Williamson refuses to compromise, and the deal doesn't go through. Neither Levene nor Williamson achieves his objective, but the dramatic agenda is set by Levene because, being the more desperate, he is the character who goes to greater extremes in the pursuit of what he wants. His energy defines the central question of the scene: Will Levene get the leads?

Scenes involving more than two characters usually place the additional people between the two dominant figures, resulting in a contest for endorsement, cooperation, loyalty, or affection of these others. In Edward Albee's *Who's Afraid of Virginia Woolf?*, for example, Honey and Nick are batted back and forth like badminton shuttles by George and Martha. To some degree, all of the characters supporting Hamlet and Claudius are defined by where they stand in relationship to the prince and his usurping uncle. In the second act of *The Odd Couple*, the Pigeon sisters are caught between Oscar's desire to put them into the mood for seduction and Felix's desire for sympathy.

In Chapter 2, I introduced the concept that the essential issues between characters could be brought to dramatic life through the negotiation over an object. In the passages just cited, characters are negotiating over *other characters*. Evidently then, the objects over which characters negotiate are not limited to inanimate physical objects. Child custody cases, for instance, are concerned with divorcing parents doing battle over with whom their children are to live. Romantic triangles find two suitors in contest for a common object of affection.

Streetcar exemplifies this principle brilliantly. In addition to all of the evocative inanimate objects over which Williams has Blanche and Stanley negotiate, the two also compete for Stella and Mitch. At the beginning of the play, both of them are firmly in Stanley's orbit. Then Blanche arrives and almost immediately calls on family feeling in an attempt to get Stella to shift primary allegiance to her. Similarly, Blanche sets her sights on Mitch, hoping to get him to turn away from his friendship with Stanley and propose marriage. Blanche's initiatives are countered by Stanley, leading to their battle for Stella and Mitch, a battle that Stanley ultimately wins.

As I suggested earlier, such negotiations by characters over other characters are likely to appear any time you have more than two characters on a stage. In Murray Schisgal's *Luv*, Harry, Ellen, and Milt are constantly passing each other back and forth. In Stephen Vincent Benét's *The Devil and Daniel Webster*, Webster and Scratch compete for the soul of Jabeez Stone. In Rodgers and Hammerstein's *Oklahoma!*, there are *two* sets of negotiations over women going on: Laurie pursued by both Curley and Jud, and Ado Annie the object of both Will's and the Peddler's attentions.

Of course, we negotiate over things other than that which we can hold or touch.

Scene from my childhood: I'm nine years old. My brother, Stuart, is six. My parents have taken us out for a drive in the family Plymouth. My parents sit in front. Stuart and I sit in the back. Inevitably:

"Mom! He hit me!"

"I didn't *hit*. I *pushed*."

"I don't want you pushing or hitting," says Mom.

"But he's on my *side*. He keeps putting his foot on my *side*."

"Do not."

"He's such a liar. You're such a liar, Stuart."

And so forth and so on because, of course, there was a border that ran right down the middle of the car. Stuart was supposed to

23

stay on his side, and I on mine, except he kept trying to infiltrate an appendage over the border onto my side—sometimes surreptitiously, under the cover of a blanket, sometimes by pretending to be asleep and sneaking an illicit toe across the vinyl upholstered no-man's-land. If, in patrolling the boundary, I found a violation, I would register my protest and plead the right to territorial integrity.

If you grew up with a sibling, this is probably a familiar scene and requires no further description. What Stuart and I were doing was negotiating over territory. Space.

Plays often deal with negotiations over space. In fact, a substantial number of plays deal with the theme of invasion.

Back to A *Streetcar Named Desire*: In addition to all of the physical objects and people over which Blanche and Stanley wrangle, they also are in a contest for the Kowalski apartment. From Stanley's perspective, Blanche is an invader, and she does what invaders often do—she asserts herself by trying to impose new rules about the use of a space where he formerly held unquestioned sway. He fights for his domain, at one point shouting, "Remember what Huey Long said—'Every Man is a King!' And I am the king around here, so don't forget it!" By the end, Stanley has reestablished the apartment as his kingdom.

Other plays in which territoriality is particularly important are Edward Albee's A *Delicate Balance*, in which Agnes and Tobias at first shelter their best friends, Edna and Harry, against some nameless dread by allowing them to become houseguests, then, finally, drive them out again; Harold Pinter's *The Homecoming*, in which the perverse wife of a college professor invades her in-laws' all-male enclave and ends up subverting both her marriage and their household; Frederick Knott's *Wait Until Dark*, in which a gang of vicious crooks trespass on the security of a blind woman's apartment; and Chekhov's *The Three Sisters*, in which Natasha marries Andrei, moves into the house he shares with the title characters, and essentially pushes them out of it (it's significant that the last act takes place outside the house).

Negotiations over space need not be on such a large scale. For instance, when I teach, I usually ask a female student to play a short scene with me. Here's the entire text:

SHE. Do you love me?
I. Yes.

The first time through, she says, "Do you love me?" and, as I say, "Yes," I move towards her.

The second time through, she says, "Do you love me?" and, as I say, "Yes," I take a step backwards.

Same text, different meaning. The difference in the meaning is due to the differences in the use of space. In the first version, the audience has some reason to believe I mean it when I say, "Yes." In the second, my retreat belies my response.

In fact, *this is what blocking is all about*. It's not just a matter of arranging things on a stage so the picture is pretty or so the audience has a clear view (though these concerns are important, too); it's about the director making manifest the relationships of the characters through the way he or she has them negotiate over space.

The meaning of a play can be transformed profoundly through the way space is used. Contrast, for instance, the Ulu Grosbard and Arvin Brown productions of David Mamet's *American Buffalo*. Under Grosbard's direction, Robert Duvall's Teach tended to claim and hold positions of strength and was all the more ominous because of it. In Brown's production, Al Pacino's Teach was all over the place, bouncing back and forth, rarely settling anywhere for more than a minute; this flightiness underscored an impression of Teach's insecurity. Both interpretations supported the text, but, because the directors had their actors use space so differently, the productions brought out distinctly different sets of meanings.

Thus far I've discussed the negotiation over space on an essentially horizontal plane. There have also been some memorable vertical negotiations, that is to say, negotiations over elevation.

In Oscar Hammerstein II's script for *The King and I*, one of the ways in which the king asserts his authority is through his insistence that nobody's head be higher than his own. Anna's challenge of his values is made physical by her resistance to the bowing he demands. At the end of the first act when he has agreed to make a significant compromise, he tests her willingness to make a reciprocal compromise by kneeling. She reluctantly kneels next to him. He lowers his head further. She lowers hers equivalently. He stretches out prone, and, with some difficulty, she matches him. To quote from the text: "They are both flat on their faces. Then he raises his head and rests his chin on his hand. She does the same. . . . Anna and the King regard each other warily. Who is taming whom?"

Shakespeare similarly uses negotiation over elevation brilliantly in *Richard* II. In Act III, scene 3, Bolingbroke, a lord in rebellion against Richard, has cornered the king in Flint Castle. Bolingbroke's emissary, Northumberland, calls up to where Richard stands on a wall, telling him that Bolingbroke is in "the base court" and desires to speak with him. "May it please you to come down?" Richard's reply:

> Down, down I come, like glist'ring Phaethon,
> Wanting the manage of unruly jades.
> In the base court? Base court, where kings grow base,
> To come at traitors' calls, and do them grace.
> In the base court? Come down? Down court! Down king!
> For night-owls shriek where mounting larks should sing.

He disappears from the wall and reappears "below," to meet Bolingbroke face-to-face. Shakespeare has vividly dramatized the metaphoric downfall of the king by bringing him down *physically*.

Timing, too, may be viewed as the way characters negotiate over time. Returning to the little scene I do with my student, depending on how swiftly I reply, "Yes," to her question, "Do you love me?" the scene may be about a man eager to proclaim his love or hesitant and probably unsure of his feelings.

There are many other things over which characters may negotiate, and *Streetcar* provides examples of most of them:

Temperature and humidity: Stanley and Blanche coping with the heat in different ways in scene 1.

Legal and other abstract or intellectual concepts: The Napoleonic Code passage in scene 2.

Sound: Blanche and Stanley fighting over the music on the radio in scene 3.

The quality and intensity of light: Mitch tearing the paper lantern off the bulb and switching on the light to get a clear look at Blanche in scene 9.

My central point is that, as in life, characters onstage negotiate over *anything* to which they attach meaning. By negotiating over inanimate objects, people, space, time, light, ideas, and other factors, characters reveal themselves and their objectives more dramatically than if they were to truthfully and overtly proclaim who they are and what they want.

4

CHAPTER

Structure

I BELIEVE THERE ARE TWO KINDS OF DRAMATIC STRUCTURE: character structure and event structure. The more common is character structure.

A character-structured work introduces a protagonist and the protagonist's overriding objective. The action of the play concerns the protagonist encountering and dealing with obstacles to this objective. In fact, the shape of the plot is *determined* by these obstacles and the resources the protagonist brings to bear in coping with them. The central question of a character-structured piece is, will the protagonist surmount the barriers and achieve his or her goal? Within minutes of the audience learning the answer to this question, the curtain should go down or the end credits should roll.

Hamlet is character-structured. Early in the play, Shakespeare establishes that Hamlet's objective is to ascertain whether the ghost is telling the truth about the death of his father and then to take the proper action, that is, kill Claudius. Despite Claudius's various intrigues against him, Hamlet prevails. The play ends (as does Hamlet himself) shortly after Hamlet achieves his vengeance.

(Incidentally, I think that Laurence Olivier hit Hamlet with a bum rap by describing him as a man who can't make up his mind. As soon as the ghost gives him an objective, Hamlet pursues it relentlessly. He throws off the balance of the court by behaving erratically; he hires the actors to put on a play to "catch the conscience of the king"; and, shortly after being satisfied by Claudius's reaction to the play that the king is indeed guilty, Hamlet makes attempts to kill him. In his first attempt, Hamlet is prevented from carrying out his intention by the fact that Claudius is praying—it being contrary to his objective of vengeance to allow Claudius to go to Heaven as Hamlet believes would happen if he were to kill him then. The second attempt results in the death of Polonius as Hamlet assumes that Claudius [and not Polonius] is hiding behind the drapes. Rather than being passive and indecisive, Hamlet is frequently and often rashly active.)

To return again to A *Streetcar Named Desire*, the central question Williams poses is whether Blanche will achieve a safe harbor. Blanche has two chances of finding this harbor: through either Stella or Mitch. The chief obstacle to her achieving her objective, of course, is Stanley. Blanche's presence constitutes a direct threat to his way of life; he responds to the threat by doing all he can to thwart her. He destroys Blanche's chances with Mitch by ferreting out Blanche's unsavory past and passing the bad word on to his friend. He destroys her chances with Stella by the rape, triggering Blanche's breakdown and her removal to a mental institution.

Yes, these analyses are patently simplistic. Obviously there is a lot more to *Hamlet* and *Streetcar* than just the question of whether Hamlet and Blanche achieve their goals. Nevertheless, both are demonstrably character-structured works.

It is especially important for the central character of a character-structured piece to have a strong objective and to take risks for it. The most memorable characters are those who are willing to indulge in the most extreme behavior in the pursuit of their goals. Though very different, Pseudolus and Sweeney Todd are the most dynamic characters in the musicals for which Stephen Sondheim has written music and lyrics, and I don't think that it's any accident that the shows they inhabit, A *Funny Thing Happened on the Way to the Forum* and *Sweeney Todd* are, dramatically speaking, Sondheim's strongest.

Early in A *Funny Thing*, it is established what Pseudolus wants above all else—his freedom. The importance of this is underscored by Sondheim giving him a song about just that—"Free."

Every prank and stratagem Pseudolus pulls during the course of the show is related directly to getting his master to give him his liberty. And, indeed, being character-structured, the show ends when Pseudolus achieves this.

Like Pseudolus, Sweeney has an all-consuming desire that he will do anything to achieve—vengeance. Sweeney gets his vengeance, of course, and shortly thereafter the show ends. As with Pseudolus, Sondheim underscores Sweeney's objective with a song, "My Friends," in which he sings to his barber's tools of the retribution he will exact with their help.

(John Guare refers to this sort of song as the "I want" song, noting that the central character usually sings it as the second song in the show. There are a fair number of exceptions to this second-song idea, but generally speaking, he's right about the "I want" song coming early on. In *My Fair Lady*, Eliza sings, "Wouldn't It Be Loverly," starting the song with the line, "All I want is a room somewhere. . . . " In the first scene of *South Pacific*, Emile sings, "This is what I need, / This is what I've longed for. . . . " In *Gypsy*, we are prepared for Rose's determination to make her mark through the song "Some People," the objective being stated—and restated throughout the show— with the line, "I had a dream. . . . ")

In contrast to *Sweeney Todd* and A *Funny Thing*, Bobby, the central character of Sondheim and George Furth's *Company*, doesn't have a clear objective until the end of the show. Not having much of an objective, he has no particular reason to act, so he doesn't. Now, I happen to love *Company*, but Bobby is so passive that he never manages to engage the audience's sympathies until the end, because, as I say, he never really *wants* anything desperately until the end, at which point he finally gets his "I want" song, "Being Alive." Fortunately for the show, he is surrounded by a stageful of people who want so much both for themselves and for him. It is *their* collective objective to solve Bobby's life for him that is the engine of the show.

The nature of the obstacles between the protagonist and the objective determines a good deal about the nature of the work. I see three different categories of obstacles—the physical obstacle, the obstacle of another character's will, and the internal obstacle, that is, something inside the character.

Adventure films best exemplify the story in which physical obstacles dominate. Will our hero climb that mountain, make it through that desert, sail that sea, coax that failing airplane back to the base, break into or out of that fortress, hack through the jungle, and blow up the enemy's bridge?

Streetcar offers an excellent example of the second category—the protagonist encountering the obstacle of another's will. As I mentioned above, Stanley's objective is the chief obstacle between Blanche and what she wants. In *Richard* II, Bolingbroke is the obstacle to Richard retaining his throne. In *The Odd Couple*, Oscar and Felix are each other's obstacles.

As for the category in which the protagonist must cope with obstacles that lie within his or her own character, I prefer to view this as a case in which the character's various roles are in collision. Chapter 6 will explore this concept at length.

In passing, let me mention that there are some character-structured plays in which there are two or more protagonists, in which case the question shifts from "Will he or she get what he or she wants?" to "Will they get what they want?" In Shaw's *Pygmalion*, for example, the ultimate question of the play is whether Higgins and Eliza will be able to make a future together after the shift in their statuses.

But not all films, TV shows, and plays are character-structured.

In the first two acts of David Storey's remarkable play *The Contractor*, a group of workers puts up a tent to be used as part of an imminent wedding reception. In the third act, the reception having occurred, they take the tent down. The play ends upon the completion of this task.

The shape of *The Contractor*, then, is not determined by a central figure pursuing a goal. (Nothing I've told you in my synopsis gives you any sense of passions driving a protagonist to compelling dramatic action.) Rather, the shape of the play is determined by an *event*. This makes *The Contractor* an event-structured piece.

An event-structured piece is one that gets its shape not from the journey of its central character or characters, but from some larger occurrence. The characters peopling the work are viewed in relation to this larger event. If a character-structured piece asks whether the protagonist will achieve a given goal, an event-structured piece asks how the overarching event in question will involve or affect the characters. In Storey's play, our acquaintance with the people in *The Contractor* is entirely through their involvement in the raising and lowering of the tent. (It should go without saying that the play is about something more than a tent. Storey uses the activity with the tent to provide the occasion for an astonishingly comprehensive view of British society at the time. I think it's a masterpiece.)

Jerome Lawrence and Robert E. Lee's *Inherit the Wind*, too, is essentially event-structured. If I were to ask you to describe this play, what would you say? "It's about a lawyer who defends a teacher over a principle of intellectual freedom"? Well, that's a fairly accurate description of the play from the lawyer's point of view, but I'd bet that most people would respond to the question along the lines of, "It's a fictionalized dramatization of the Scopes trial." By saying so, they've named the event that gives the play its structure: the trial. The first act is the preparation for the trial. The second act concentrates on the testimony given, culminating in the scene in which the defense attorney (based on Clarence Darrow) puts the star prosecutor (based on William Jennings Bryan) on the stand. The third act focuses on the verdict and the immediate consequences of the trial.

This is not to say that there aren't fully drawn characters. The two attorneys are titanic presences and consequently have attracted major stars in the script's various incarnations on stage, film, and television. The point I'm making, however, is that the structure that *contains* these characters is the trial. Sitting out front, we know that the end of the trial will cue the end of the play.

A trial is a natural form for drama, which is one of the reasons why there are so many plays and films based on trials. The first trial play we know of was Aeschylus's *The Eumenides*, the third play in the *Orestia*. Among the other trial dramas that come to mind: Tom Topor's *Nuts*, Agatha Christie's *Witness for the Prosecution*, Father Daniel Berrigan's *The Trial of the Catonsville Nine*, and Saul Levitt's *The Andersonville Trial*. Some of these plays stick strictly to scenes in the courtroom, others show us a bit of the life of the characters outside of the court, but all of these plays end very shortly after the verdict or judgment has been announced. This is true also of films about trials: *The Verdict*, *Judgment at Nuremberg*, *Breaker Morant*, and *Anatomy of a Murder*. The central event being concluded, the show ends. (In fact, one of the problems with Herman Wouk's otherwise admirable play *The Caine Mutiny Court-Martial* is that the form of the script signals the audience to believe that the evening will be over upon the announcement of the verdict. At the performances I've seen of it, when the lights came up again after that announcement, the audience began to applaud what they expected was a curtain call. It was only after several seconds that they realized that there was to be an epilogue that takes place in a hotel room. The result was much confusion and mumbling.)

Many event-structured pieces are based on other formal, clearly defined rituals. Robert Altman's film *A Wedding* takes its shape from the title ceremony and the subsequent reception. Jules Feiffer's *The White House Murder Case* is in the form of a meeting between the President and his cabinet. The occasion of Christopher Durang's *Sister Mary Ignatius Explains It All to You* is a lecture to the audience by the title character.

This is not to say that the event in an event-structured script has to be what is normally recognized as a formal occasion like a trial, a wedding reception, a cabinet meeting, or a lecture. An event-structured script may be based on any event the shape of which is sensed by the audience as encompassing a complete action.

A whole genre of film is based on event structure—the disaster movie. Look at *The Towering Inferno*. Its structure can be outlined swiftly: part one shows how the fire starts, part two, how it goes out of control, and part three, how it is fought and subdued. The movie ends when the fire is extinguished. In line with what I said above, our interest in the characters in *The Towering*

Inferno focuses on how they are affected by the fire; we watch to find out which stars will survive.

If you're having trouble trying to decide whether a piece you're developing is character- or event-structured, ask yourself the question, "What is this play about?" If your answer begins, "It's about this guy who . . . " or "It's about this woman who . . . , " you're fairly certain to be facing character structure. But if you answer, "It's about a court-martial," or "It's about a plot to blow up an ocean liner," odds are you're plowing another field. Notice I was able to describe the central action of *The Towering Inferno* without mentioning any of the characters. If you can tell someone what a movie or a play is about without reference to individual characters, you're almost certainly dealing with an event-structured piece. It's also worth noting that event-structured scripts tend to feature a larger cast of characters than do those that are character-structured.

Now that I've used those terms to the point at which I'm sure you never want to see them repeated, here they come again:

Just as a play or a film may be analyzed as having a character or event structure, so also may individual scenes within a script be analyzed as being character- or event-structured. Thus an event-structured piece will include character-structured scenes and a character-structured piece may include event-structured scenes.

For instance, I classified *Hamlet* as a character-structured play, but there are event-structured scenes within *Hamlet*: the presentation of the play-within-the-play, Ophelia's funeral, and the fencing match between Hamlet and Laertes. The *shapes* of all these scenes are determined by the formal conventions of the performance of a play, a funeral, and a fencing match. (In all of these cases, the formal conventions are violated, but I'll get to that in a later chapter.)

Kramer vs. Kramer is also character-structured. It efficiently introduces Dustin Hoffman's character: a Manhattan advertising man whose wife abandons him and his son and who soon establishes his objective—to build and sustain a secure and loving relationship with the boy. This objective is threatened when ex-wife Meryl Streep reappears seeking custody. The picture ends when Hoffman achieves his goal and retains custody of the son. In the middle of this character-structured movie, there is a sustained sequence shaped by the event to which the action of the film has been building—the custody hearing. The sequence concludes when the judge renders his judgment.

As for an example of an event-structured piece containing character-structured scenes, let's go back to Inherit the Wind. At one point, the defendant's girlfriend tries to persuade the defendant to give up his stand on principle. The defendant's lawyer, Drummond, tries to keep him from doing so. The structure of the scene is keyed to whether or not the girlfriend achieves her objective. (Of course she doesn't, otherwise there would be no trial. No trial, no event. No event, no Inherit the Wind.)

One bravura passage in Bertoit Brecht's Galileo features a sequence in which the Pope mulls over how to deal with the title character while, in wordless counterpoint, assorted minions assist him in putting on the elaborate costume of his position. At the beginning, he is seen standing in his underclothes. By the end, he is fully attired for his role a Prince of the Church. In fact, this scene is commonly referred to as "the robing scene."

Each individual beats in a script may be event-structured. A technique that often gives a passage particular brilliance sets a physical activity with a predetermined shape (a beginning, middle, and end) in counterpoint to the dialogue, or vice versa.

In the first scene of Edmond Rostand's Cyrano de Bergerac, Cyrano enters into a duel announcing that at the same time he is fencing, he intends to extemporaneously compose a sonnet, and the duel will end as he finishes his composition. And, indeed, as he finds his last rhyme, he thrusts home. By setting up the device of improvising the poem, Rostand gives an extra shape and tension to what might have been just another stage fight.

Sometimes a talented actor or director will some up with stage business that will function in this way. Richard Monette's 1992 production of Romeo and Juliet at Ontario's Stratford Festival featured just such a bit. At one point, Colm Feore as Mercutio placed his foil on the stage and gave it a tap. While it rolled on its guard in a circle around the tip, he paced a speech so that the grip returned to its starting position just in time for him to snatch it up on the last word. (Just the sort of bravura stunt the show-off Mercutio would pull.) The event of the foil's revolution reinforced the shape of the passage.

It's wonderful to work with directors and actors who are so resourceful as to come up with touches like this, but I see no reason dramatists can't initiate such devices in the writing. One of my students wrote a particularly effective scene in which a gangster tried to remember his list of six errands as he loaded six bullets into a pistol, using the bullets as mnemonic devices. There was a little flush of delight in the audience as it realized the connection between the physical and the mental activities.

I recognize that few people are likely to start a project by saying, "I want to write a character-structured play," or "I feel a burning desire to do an event-structured film." In my experience, scripts spring from less abstract impulses. But once you've chosen your subject, determining which of these structures will better serve your material will help you figure out how to tell your story.

About Characters

ONCE IN A WHILE, LIFE OFFERS A MOMENT OF PERFECT DRAMA.

In 1954, Senator Joseph McCarthy accuses the U.S. Army of being riddled with Communist infiltrators. Congressional hearings are organized, with Joseph N. Welch acting as special counsel for the Army. On June 9, in an attempt to gain an advantage, McCarthy rises in front of live television cameras to smear the reputation of Fred Fisher, one of the younger lawyers associated with Welch's law firm, by revealing Fisher's short-lived affiliation with a left-leaning organization.

Quietly, Welch responds, "Until this moment, Senator, I think I never really gauged your cruelty or your recklessness. Fred Fisher is a young man who went to the Harvard Law School and came into my firm and is starting what looks to be a brilliant career with us. . . . Little did I dream you could be so reckless and so cruel as to do an injury to that lad."

McCarthy tries to rally a reply, but Welch cuts him off, saying, "Let us not assassinate this lad further, Senator. You have done enough. Have you no sense of decency, sir, at long last? Have you no sense of decency?"

These simple, extraordinary, powerful words help bring to their end both Joe McCarthy and the era to which he lent his name. A moment in life that matches the power of a great stage confrontation.

And it is all the rarer for being so. Mostly, the conflicts in life do not play out so elegantly. Mostly, people do not rise to the occasion with a spontaneous burst of devastating eloquence. Rather, in the pressure of the moment, they stumble and stammer, repeat themselves a lot, garbling grammar and syntax in the process. The indisputable truth is that life is messy. Its events do not tend to occur in well-proportioned, aesthetically pleasing scenes.

And this is one of the reasons many playwrights write plays—to improve on life. To bring order—motivation, cause and effect, and erudition—to the anarchy, herky-jerkiness, and inarticulateness of reality.

Many plays are born out of the authors' desire to summon up central contests in their lives and replay them with the benefit of authorial control, control that they did not possess as participants in the events—how wonderfully therapeutic! Life has the frustrating habit of going its own way and dragging you with it. As a playwright, the life you create for the stage goes *your* way. You can humiliate the villains and reward virtue, dispensing God-like justice. Talk about a sense of empowerment!

But this impulse to forge drama out of the vicissitudes of one's own life much more often than not leads to seriously flawed plays, so much so that I strongly advise students to avoid writing autobiographical plays.

Before I get to reasons, an anecdote:

In *Shake Well Before Using*, Bennett Cerf quoted Laurence Olivier on a backstage incident during a run of Shaw's *Arms and the Man* in which Olivier was playing Sergius. Director Tony Guthrie stopped by to say hello, and Olivier started to gripe about what a problem he was having with the role. Guthrie asked Olivier, "But don't you love Sergius?" Olivier exploded. How could *anyone* love Sergius—a conformist who does little but provide the cues for others' witticisms? Guthrie's reply: "Well, of course, if you can't love Sergius, you'll never be any good in him, will you?" Olivier credited Guthrie's comment with helping him reach a breakthrough as an actor.

This is another of those instances in which something that applies to the actor's craft applies to the writer's. If you somehow can't muster love for your characters—*all* of your characters, including the antagonists—you're unlikely to write them well.

What does this have to do with the pitfalls of autobiographically inspired writing? As I said above, the autobiographic play often is born out of the impulse to impose authorial control on an event from real life. This usually leads to a scenario in which the character standing in for the author endures slings and arrows launched by other people, which, in turn, automatically makes those other people either evil or stupid.

To write a play assuming from the word go that all but the character based on you are SOB's or ignoramuses makes it very difficult to muster the love for those other characters you need to write them well.

Let's take a hypothetical example. Say you're a man whose girlfriend has dumped you for someone else. If you try to write a play about this, your natural perspective is going to be that (1) she should have stayed with you because you are a superior person and (2) she shouldn't have hooked up with the other guy because he's shallow or evil or otherwise unworthy. Logically, then, the lady in question has done something incredibly WRONG, which means she is probably deluded or corrupt or otherwise profoundly flawed.

So here are your characters: the one based on you—possessing an essentially noble nature, though probably adept at tart quips to cover your wounded feelings; the one based on your rival—undoubtedly a snake or dork of some stripe; and the one based on the woman—attractive in some way, certainly (or you wouldn't have been attracted to her in the first place), but compromised by some terrible character deficiency.

Given your feelings for the real-life people, how likely is it you'll give their dramatic counterparts a fair shake in your play? How likely will the resulting parts be characters the actors playing them will be able to love?

Because, yes, you do have to be concerned about this. Actors have to give life to your characters, so you have to give them some way of playing even your villains and dolts from the inside, creating alliances with their souls. *Richard* III, for instance, is an actor's favorite. He may be a hypocritical, murderous monster, but he has such vitality and bravado, such a thrillingly wicked wit, that actors relish playing him. He appeals to the gremlin in each of us.

In contrast, actors rarely get much pleasure out of playing Nick in Edward Albee's *Who's Afraid of Virginia Woolf?* because it's obvious that Albee himself doesn't like or enjoy Nick. (George Segal in the film is the only actor I've seen triumph in the part; he made Nick's surliness seem like a rebellion against George's condescension.)

Let me now throw in a joker: You don't have to worry about a point of sympathy when you're dealing with farce and the far fringes of melodrama. In neither form are we terribly concerned about believability of characterization. Heroes are heroes and villains are villains. They exist not to reveal any interior life to the audience but to keep the plot going. The actor who is concerned about finding a way to get inside Moriarty in William Gilette's *Sherlock Holmes* is running contrary to the intentions of the piece. Farce and melodrama are not primarily about the subtleties of characterization but about situation.

Neither are they concerned with credibility. The James Bond films, for example, are a mixture of farce and melodrama, and not one of them is remotely believable. But that's not what's important. What's important is that the action be engaging, and we in the audience are happy to make a contract with the creators whereby we suspend normal standards of credibility in return for a good time.

Just as the plots of farce and melodrama don't have to be believable, so the characters that people them don't have to be believable in the same way that they do in plays—whether comedy or drama—that make some attempt at portraying a credible picture of the way people behave. In a farce, for instance, we'll accept an actor running on in a fright wig telling us he's the world's greatest scientist because, as I say, we don't hold farce to the same standards we apply when watching *Death of a Salesman* or *The Glass Menagerie*.

To return to the subject of autobiographic writing, I have another reason for discouraging it:

For some reason, we think of ourselves as acted upon rather than acting. You are more likely to say, "Something interesting *happened* to me today," than, "I *did* something interesting today." This habit of perceiving yourself as being on the receiving end of events doesn't serve you very well in creating a character based on yourself because you tend to transfer to that character this passive mode.

Autobiographic characters are almost always the most passive characters onstage. They tend to observe and comment wryly off to the side rather than kick things off.

The various plays and movies based on Christopher Isherwood's *Berlin Stories* consistently ran into trouble with the character based on Isherwood himself. The source of the problem is hinted by the title of the first dramatization, the stage play I *Am a Camera*. When looking at a photograph, one doesn't think much of the camera that took the picture, one thinks of the subject in the picture. And so it is with the Isherwood character, who is present mostly to witness. The character is so ill defined that from version to version his name kept getting changed. In I *Am a Camera*, playwright John Van Druten retained Isherwood's name. In *Cabaret* onstage, the author of the book, Joseph Masteroff, calls him Cliff Bradshaw. In the film version, written by Jay Presson Allen, he is dubbed Brian Roberts. I think the character is most successfully drawn in this last version, but still he is the most restrained character in the picture. It is Sally Bowles in her feverish pursuit of what she thinks is the good life who is the most dynamic presence and consequently the best remembered.

Similarly, in *Long Day's Journey into Night*, Edmund, the character Eugene O'Neill based upon himself, is easily the least dynamic of the four principals. And in Neil Simon's trilogy, *Brighton Beach Memoirs*, *Biloxi Blues*, and *Broadway Bound*, while Simon's alter ego Eugene Jerome does a lot of entertaining editorializing to the audience, when it comes to the dramatic action, all of the other characters are more vital than he is. I wonder if it is for this reason, to justify Eugene's passivity, that in the second act of *Broadway Bound* Simon gives Eugene an energy-sapping case of the flu.

Their stand-ins' passivity notwithstanding, O'Neill's and Simon's plays still work. Both dramatists drew on reservoirs of acquired craft to offset most of the inherent perils of autobio-graphic writing.

But new writers generally don't have the resources to deal with these pitfalls. The result usually is a play in which the central character suffers much undeserved bad luck and whines about it a lot. Worse yet, being a passive character, he or she doesn't do much of anything except react. With the central character constitutionally incapable of driving the plot forward, the play tends to lack dramatic action.

But, you say, something happened to you that you *have* to make a play out of.

OK, if you *have* to . . .

My advice is to so transform the character based on yourself that you cease to think of him or her as representing you. Change the gender, change the sex, change the age, change the nationality—anything that will give the character a life in your mind independent from your own history, perspective, and grievances. Odds are you will be less worried about making all of that character's behavior attractive or writing a lot of special pleading on his or her behalf. At the point at which the character does something you would never *dream* of doing, you will have won the battle, though not necessarily the war.

For the same reason many dramatists write autobiographic characters, they are tempted to make characters writers. Unfortunately, making the lead character a writer is almost as problematic as giving the lead to an autobiographic figure.

It is not as great a problem in a novel. Novels tend to place more emphasis on perception than on action; they depict more thought processes and philosophy and less behavior. Certainly this seems to be the case with many of the great novels, which is why they resist dramatization. Nobody would claim, for instance, that the film version of *The Brothers Karamazov* provides an experience equivalent to reading the novel. But novels concentrating on behavior rather than on perception are easily dramatized, which is why a second-rate novel like *The Godfather* can be transformed into a pair of film classics (I'm referring to the first two *Godfather* pictures; I don't think the third one matches them). Children's stories, with their emphasis on action, also translate to dramatic form well; witness all of the dramatizations of the Grimms' fairy tales and the perennial success of *The Wizard of Oz*.

As I say, a novel can delve into a character's perceptions and thought processes, and this can be fascinating on the page. But trying to translate such a character (who in a novel spends most of his or her time commenting on the other characters or telling us of his or her perceptions of nature or some such) into a dramatic character is very difficult. Unless a clever dramatist can imply this character's perceptions through behavior, such a character is not likely to register onstage or onscreen with anything like the impact he or she had on the page.

Take, for example, the character of Stingo in *Sophie's Choice*. In William Styron's book, we get to know him very well because everything we learn is filtered through his perceptions, the by-product of the interaction between his intelligence and the people and events he observes. Because of these perceptions, in the book we believe he is indeed a writer.

But in Alan J. Pakula's conscientious film adaptation, despite some voice-over material attributed to the grown Stingo and despite what I think is a fine performance by Peter MacNicol, Stingo hardly registers dramatically. He is there simply to have things revealed to him. Except for when he tries to help Sophie escape from Nathan, which is very late in the story, he does nothing to influence the course of events. Nor does he do anything to lend credence to him being a writer.

But then I don't believe Jane Fonda is a writer in *Julia*. And I don't believe Frank Sinatra is a writer in *Some Came Running*. And I don't believe the guy in *Chapter Two* is a writer (a widower yes, but not a writer), or that Diane Keaton is capable of writing greeting card verse, much less *New Yorker*–quality poetry, in *Interiors*, or that Robin Williams is a serious novelist in *The World According to Garp*. And in 1776, I don't for a second buy that Ken Howard is writing the Declaration of Independence.

I think it is almost impossible to believably characterize a writer dramatically. What behavior can one observe that *proves* someone is a writer? The true work of writing is not socially observable; it happens inside one's head. All you can show is the external behavior of a writer, which is why plays and films about writers almost always feature some variation of the following scene:

> *Late at night. Writer sits at cluttered desk. A half-smoked cigarette in the ash tray. A cup of coffee or perhaps some booze at hand. In front of our subject, a typewriter or a pile of blank sheets of paper and a pen. Fade in, writer is knitting brows. Takes a drag from the cigarette. Makes a face. It doesn't have the kick it should. Gets an idea, begins to scribble. Apparently the idea peters out. Crosses out a line or two. Takes a drink of the cold coffee or a sip of the booze. Makes another face. Takes another stab at writing a few lines. Stops, looks at what has been written. Crosses out some more. Then crumples up the page in disgust.*

Faced with having to write this scene in *Julia*, Alvin Sargent took it one step further and had Jane Fonda toss her typewriter out the window.

But what does all this coffee drinking and scribbling and face making prove to an audience? Merely that the character can make marks on a page, grimace, drink, and smoke. (The only novelist I've ever believed in a play is Trigorin in *The Seagull*. When played by the right actor, I do believe that Trigorin writes fiction. Second-rate fiction, perhaps, but fiction nonetheless. I am frankly mystified by how Chekhov pulled this off.)

Generally speaking, the only writer I think has much chance of being believably characterized in a dramatic piece is a journalist. This is because in newspaper stories we see almost nothing of the writing process itself. Rather, in *The Front Page*, *All the President's Men*, and *Lou Grant*, we see the *social* aspect of being a journalist—the tactics and stratagems of getting information from other people.

This leads me to suggest that the professions that best lend themselves to characterization on the stage and screen are those that by definition call for interaction with other people. If you accept the idea that scenes consist of negotiations among characters, obviously you are at a dramatic advantage if the characters' professions by definition involve engagement with others. A novelist's work being essentially private and solitary, making your central character a novelist automatically places a hindrance to interaction between him/her and the other characters.

So, what sorts of professions do lend themselves to drama?

Well, I think it is no accident there have been so many plays and movies with teachers as key characters. *Pygmalion*, of course. *Butley*; *Life Class*; *Open Admissions*; *Eminent Domain*; *The Corn Is Green*; *To Sir with Love*; *Who's Afraid of Virginia Woolf?*; *Blackboard Jungle*; *Conrack*; *The Miracle Worker*; *The Wild Child*; *Goodbye, Mr. Chips*; *The Browning Version*; *Child's Play*; *The Lesson*; and so on.

There are also tons of plays and films about doctors, cops, politicians, soldiers, prostitutes, the clergy, royalty, private eyes, psychiatrists, and athletes. All of these professions involve socially observable behavior, behavior that necessitates the presence of and interaction with other characters.

It's no accident that most TV series are keyed to the leading characters' jobs. A profession automatically gives a character an objective, so coming up with stories is merely a matter of coming up with a series of professional challenges. We know with *The Rockford Files* or *Harry O* that in each episode the detective will be faced with a case to solve. On *Trapper John, M. D.*, MASH, and *St. Elsewhere*, the doctors will face a never-ending supply of medical emergencies. On L.A. *Law*, *Law and Order*, and *Reasonable Doubt*, the attorneys will be hit with new legal problems.

Still, because novelists continue to write some very good novels about novelists and some of these books make the bestseller list and get sold to the movies, we will continue to see disappointing movies based on them. We will continue to see pictures like *Garp* and *Sophie's Choice*, and critics and audiences will continue to badmouth the acting of those actors trapped into playing parts like Garp and Stingo, not recognizing that it's almost impossible to convincingly *play* a novelist or a poet.

In addition to the professions and natures of the characters in your play, you must be concerned about how many you have. The number of characters in your play will necessarily determine a great deal about the kind of play you write. Look at the plays that are packed with plenty of story—*Nicholas Nickleby*, *Detective Story*, *The Little Foxes*, all of Shakespeare—and you'll notice that they demand sizeable casts. Look, in contrast, to plays with under a half-dozen characters, and you'll see that, instead of densely packed narrative, you get works long on nuance and personal revelation. Small-cast plays tend to be about the beginnings or endings of relationships (*Frankie and Johnny in the Claire de Lune*, *'night, Mother*) or internal warfare in families.

There's nothing about cast size that precludes the possibility of greatness. *Who's Afraid of Virginia Woolf?*, *Long Day's Journey into Night* and *The Glass Menagerie* are among the most powerful works our theater has produced, and the largest of these requires a cast of five.

But I think it is demonstrably true that smaller-cast plays are harder to write. The fewer characters onstage, the fewer mathematical possibilities there are for issues to settle, the more ingenuity required to sustain interest for a full evening.

Let's assume you have a three-character play featuring Albert, Becky, and Charles. Here are the possible combinations for scenes: (1) Albert, Becky, and Charles; (2) Albert and Becky; (3) Albert and Charles; (4) Becky and Charles; (5) Albert solo; (6) Becky solo; and (7) Charles solo.

Now, let's posit a two-character play featuring Dana and Enid. The possible combinations: (1) Dana and Enid; (2) Dana solo; and (3) Enid solo.

So with one fewer character, you have fewer than half the possibilities for scenes than you had with three. And let's face it, solo scenes in a two-character play tend to be kind of a drag. Either you stick the actor with the less-than-enviable task of talking to the audience or to him- or herself, or you whip up a scene with a telephone, trying to make one half of a conversation sound credible and interesting.

The challenge of a two-character play is that, by definition, there is essentially one issue to be resolved between two characters, and it's very hard to sustain a contest over one issue for a full evening of theater. So, much of the time, two-character plays feel stretched out, padded.

Frequently the playwright employs a delaying tactic. An early scene in Vincent J. Cardinal's *The Colorado Catechism*, for instance, depicts a painter arriving at an institution designed to help people deal with substance abuses. He encounters a woman who represents herself as being a nurse. "Represents" is the key word, for, after a fairly long dialogue between them, she reveals that she is a fellow patient.

I don't doubt that Cardinal, who, incidentally, is a writer of talent, could come up with a spirited defense of the scene. But watching it, it looked to me as if the imposture were there mainly to put off for a while the time when the two actually face each other as themselves. The rest of the play—dealing with the relationship between these two patients over the period of the next several weeks—would not have been appreciably different in its impact minus this scene, only shorter.

Ira Lewis's *Chinese Coffee* also employs delaying tactics. The issue to be settled between the two characters concerns a novel that down-at-his-heels Harry Levine has written that paints a portrait of his friendship with photographer Jacob Manheim to which Manheim objects. But, except for a passing reference early on to establish the manuscript's existence, about half of the play's ninety-minute, intermissionless length goes by before the battle over the novel is joined. (I must confess, I found the delay more interesting than the battle. But a delay it still was.)

Another technique to which crafty dramatists have resorted to make a two-hander hold stage for a full evening is to employ a temporal gimmick to render the script virtually a series of related one-acts.

Bernard Slade's *Same Time, Next Year* is about a man and a woman who sustain an extramarital relationship over a period of twenty-five years, meeting in a motel one weekend annually. Each of the two acts is made up of three scenes, each scene taking place five years later than the previous one. The *raison d'être* of the play is to use these two people as indirect reflections of the history and changing social mores outside the motel.

Each scene we wait to discover how the intervening years have transformed them, watching their clothes, hairstyles, and attitudes shift as the decades pass. The shy housewife becomes something of a flower child. The mild-mannered guy becomes an anal-retentive conservative. And then, when we catch them five years later, they're each someone else.

And that's why Slade has enough matter with which to occupy our attention for two hours plus: The changes in their characters and the times are sufficient to give them six different sets of subissues to cope with over the course of the evening. Though there is a larger arc to the story, each scene has its own complete little tale to tell. Each has exposition to expose, conflicting objectives to establish, and action leading to resolution until the next scene raises a new brace of concerns.

Jan de Hartog's *The Fourposter*, which was the basis of the Harvey Schmidt and Tom Jones musical I D*o! I Do!*, operates on a similar premise. With the fourposter bed as a constant presence, the script follows a wife and husband from their first days of marriage through early problems, then the threat of his affair with another woman, and ultimately to contentment in old age. Again, each scene takes place significantly later than the previous one so that they have new problems to solve each time the lights come up again.

Anthony Shaffer found another way round the two-character limitation in his suspense classic, *Sleuth*. (If you don't know the play, skip this paragraph until you've seen or read it.) At the end of the first act, we're led to believe that one of the characters has murdered the other. At the beginning of the second act, an Inspector Doppler appears to investigate. Except he isn't an inspector at all. After a long scene of thrust and parry between Doppler and the suspected murderer, Doppler pulls off his makeup to reveal himself as the man the audience has been led to believe was a murder victim. By this ruse, Shaffer not only threw in a neat plot twist, he also added the texture and a scenic possibility that a real third character would have introduced.

I'm not claiming it's impossible to write a full-length two-actor play without padding or resorting to a time or disguise gimmick (or, as in Amlin Gray's *How I Got That Story*, having one of the two actors play a variety of characters) I have a high opinion of D. L. Coburn's *The Gin Game*, which doesn't feel padded and doesn't leap years from scene to scene. And I'm sure many would also nominate Marsha Norman's *'night, Mother* for inclusion on the short honor roll.

But a theater limited to plays requiring only a handful of actors is a theater whose range of subject matter is, by definition, limited. It is hard to present a story dealing with the collision of large social forces if you don't put enough people on the stage to represent those forces. Jerome Lawrence and Robert E. Lee's *Inherit the Wind* and Howard Sackler's *The Great White Hope* (both of which are lightly fictionalized dramatizations of history) wouldn't have the same impact if the writers hadn't brought substantial ensembles onto the stage representing the societies whose values create the contexts for the central characters' struggles. For that matter, it is hard to do a show that explores a milieu in a quasi-sociological way without a large enough group to embody it. Try to imagine getting the story of Hecht and MacArthur's *The Front Page* onstage without the gang of reporters and the large supporting cast of cops, corrupt politicians, and the other Chicago types that lend that classic comedy much of its color. Try to imagine O'Neill's *The Iceman Cometh* as a piece for two or three actors.

As a result, few nonmusical American plays today possess a sense of grandeur. It is dismaying that the American theater has so little room for large, straight plays. Indeed, they seem to be impossible to undertake without the promise of corporate underwriting. I think this is a shame.

These days, the smaller the cast, the more attractive theaters find a project. Here's the catch:

The practical playwright understands the odds against getting a large-scale project produced, so instead, most of us write small-cast works.

This isn't to say that writing a large-cast play is a breeze. (Little about dramatic writing is a breeze.) In a small-cast play, as there are few characters, the audience has no difficulty in keeping them straight. Writing a large-cast piece, you're faced with the problem of making each of your major characters a distinct presence.

Back when I was researching *Something Wonderful Right Away*, I sat in on a session at Second City during which, based on a suggestion from the audience, the company improvised a scene about a bunch of colorfully corrupt Chicago politicians at a political dinner. Later that evening, after the audience was gone, Bernard Sahlins, who was then both producing and directing, discussed with the company how to reshape the scene so that it might have a future. His chief observation was that since the scene began with all of these characters on the stage at the dinner, the audience found it difficult to figure out who was who. Sahlins's suggestion was that the scene be reorganized so that the characters make separate entrances and that each entrance present the character in an action that made a specific and vivid impression. And, indeed, when the company attempted to do the scene again, the separate entrances and introductions made the characters easier to follow in the ensemble scene that followed.

In A *Midsummer Night's Dream*, Shakespeare gives the various groups of characters separate introductory sections—the quartet of young fugitive lovers get their own scene; the mechanicals are introduced in their own scene; the fairy royalty, Oberon and Titania, and their attendants, too, are established in a distinct section. Having gone to pains to introduce each group and the internal politics of each, Shakespeare then feels confident about proceeding with action in which the three groups collide and interact. The fact that the audience is able to keep the characters straight during the hectic action that is the bulk of the play is the result of the care with which Shakespeare has established them separately.

Look, too, at Peter Stone's book for the musical 1776. The action of this show involves the complex interweave of motives of some twenty members of the Continental Congress. To create a circumstance by which he may fix the identity of each of the twenty clearly in the audience's mind, in scene 3, Stone introduces Dr. Lyman Hall, a delegate newly arrived from Georgia. During the course of the subsequent fifteen minutes or so, Hall meets the other nineteen as they make their staggered entrances.

Stephen Hopkins of Rhode Island comes roaring on demanding rum and proclaiming his eminence by virtue of his age. Edward Rutledge, the young, handsome, and aristocratic delegate from South Carolina tries to recruit Hall to his position by invoking the unity of the South. The three members of the Delaware delegation enter arguing furiously among themselves, setting up the internal tensions that will pay off dramatically later. Pennsylvania delegate John Dickinson asks Caesar Rodney, one of the Delaware delegates, to introduce him to Hall saying, "I trust, Caesar, when you're through converting the poor fellow to independency that you'll give the opposition a fair crack at him." This neatly establishes both Rodney's position and Dickinson's. Dickinson's associate, James Wilson, clears his throat to signal that Rodney has neglected to introduce *him* to Hall. Rodney replies, "Ah, Judge Wilson, forgive me—but how can anyone see you if you insist on standing in Mr. Dickinson's shadow?" This line adroitly and succinctly characterizes the relationship between Dickinson and Wilson, which will be of crucial importance at the show's climax. These gentlemen are followed onto the stage by Ben Franklin, whose painfully gouty leg cannot dampen his humor. ("I only wish King George felt like my big toe—all over!")

And so on, until all twenty delegates are onstage. By the end of the scene, a member of the audience cannot claim to know them in great depth, but the vignettes through which they have been brought on have established the dramatic equivalent of ID tags so that one can distinguish among them. (It is scenes such as this that make Stone's work on 1776 justifiably among the most admired books in American musical theater.)

So, yes, large-cast plays offer their own technical challenges, but still, I'd much rather have a stage full of characters buzzing around, full of energy and contradictory objectives to generate a full evening's worth of story. If only more producers could afford to put shows of this scale on.

6
CHAPTER
Roles in Conflict

IN CHAPTER 4, I THEORIZED THAT THERE ARE THREE CLASSES OF obstacles a character may encounter: (1) physical obstacles; (2) obstacles produced by other characters' wills; and (3) obstacles within the character. In this chapter, I want to explore the idea of how drama may spring from this third class.

I don't want to hear any excuses. Pick up your room or I'm not taking you to see the Mets play.

You tell us that they were married for seven years, but you have them explaining things to each other as if they were strangers. Even if they haven't seen each other for several months, they would still have a shorthand between them.

I swear to you, nobody ever lost a writing job because of what their shirt looked like. But if it will make you happy, I'll get everything dry-cleaned before I go to the studio.

Three different voices. The first, speaking to my son. The second, to a student. The third, to my mother. All three voices recognizably mine, yet distinct.

The point?

Sometimes you hear writers talking about finding a character's voice, but I find it more useful to think of the character's *voices*. For, as I've demonstrated, we do not speak the same to all people. Rather, we employ different voices with different people as appropriate.

Each different voice represents a different role. To my son, I speak as a father; to my student, as a teacher; to my mother, as a son who will never learn the value of a good wardrobe.

Shaw once said that the drama of a man's life arises when his professional life comes into conflict with his private life. I think he was on to something (he usually was), but I would extend the idea. I believe that the drama of one's life is the product of a conflict between two or more roles that are both of enormous importance but are ultimately irreconcilable. To extend this from the realm of psychology to drama, I find that many of the plays and films I admire are based on such conflicts in the souls of their protagonists.

Billy Wilder and I. A. L. Diamond's screenplay for *The Apartment* (which also served as the basis for Neil Simon's script for the musical *Promises, Promises*) concerns one C. C. Baxter (played by Jack Lemmon), an employee at a New York insurance company. Within short order, Wilder and Diamond deftly set up Baxter's two sides.

On the one hand, Baxter has a hunger to succeed, to climb the corporate ladder to an executive position. In pursuit of his goal, he goes so far as to lend his apartment for extramarital hanky-panky to executives who might help him advance. This establishes one of his roles: the morally equivocal careerist.

Baxter has other hopes. Every day, on his way up to work, he trades pleasantries with an attractive, spirited, young elevator operator named Fran (Shirley MacLaine). The fact is he is smitten with her. His intentions are good, but being somewhat shy, he hasn't quite worked up the courage to articulate them. He hasn't even worked up the courage to call her by her first name, addressing her always as Miss Kubelik. His second role: the honorable would-be suitor.

The action of *The Apartment* concerns the collision between the morally equivocal careerist and the honorable suitor, for Baxter discovers that the lady his boss Jeff Sheldrake (Fred Mac-Murray) has been bedding in his (Baxter's) apartment is Miss Kubelik. One night he returns home and finds Fran in his bed, passed out from a suicide attempt. Now the battle between his two roles is joined. He reaches the point at which he cannot advance his career and maintain his honor (and thus, in our eyes, deserve to win Miss Kubelik's heart). The choice he makes—to be a *mensch* and walk away from the cynical values by which he has risen—determines the path he will follow thereafter. The choice he makes then sets up a choice for Fran to make which, in turn, makes their future together possible.

The Apartment, then, is a fairly pure example of a script based on the dramatic dynamic I outlined above. At its simplest, a piece based on this dynamic must introduce a character, identify two deeply held but mutually exclusive roles, and then move to a point at which this character must choose between these roles. Which role the character chooses then determines that character's fate.

Notice I say "*deeply held* but mutually exclusive roles." If there aren't compelling reasons for the central character to seriously consider *each*, then there is no contest between the roles. If there's no contest, then there's no tension and probably no drama. *The Apartment* wouldn't be the extraordinary picture it is if it weren't for the fact that Baxter wants to be successful in business *almost* as much as he wants to win Fran's love. The body of *The Apartment* delineates the process by which he realizes the nature of the choice he has to make.

More examples:

The two characters in Athol Fugard's *The Blood Knot* are half-brothers—one black, the other capable of passing for white. Their fraternal roles generate one type of relationship; their racial roles generate another. The action of the play describes the circumstances under which the antagonistic relationship imposed by South African society threatens the loving fraternal one.

Hamlet is about a particularly traumatic collision of roles. The behavior mandated by Hamlet's role as his father's son is in wrenching contrast to what is expected of him as his mother's son. His duties as a prince are in conflict with his impulses as Ophelia's lover. The acting coach he plays as he talks to the players is different from the potential suicide portrayed in soliloquy. Among Hamlet's problems is coping with the pull of these different roles. (In fact, in fulfilling his obligations as avenger, he finds it necessary to create yet another role to serve as camouflage—the madman; since a madman is not held accountable to the rules of logical behavior, it is a role that allows him great latitude in pursuing Claudius.) His choice to be his father's avenger above all other options makes impossible any chance of fulfilling any of the other roles. (Of course, it's pretty hard for him to fulfill any other roles when he and almost everyone of consequence to him lie dead at the play's end.)

Comic plays, too, may find their source in the conflict that lies within their central characters' souls. In *The Odd Couple*, for instance, Oscar's role as Felix's friend leads him to take on the role of Felix's roommate. The action of the play is the revelation of the ways in which being his roommate threatens the friendship.

The title character of Molière's *Tartuffe* professes to be a devout and honorable man, abjuring wealth and fleshly temptation. Molière's concern is with the revelation of Tartuffe's true character. It is the proof of the disparity between what he professes to be in public and what he proves to be in private that leads to his deserved downfall.

A common theme running through all of these plays is the central characters' discovery of their true roles and what befalls them when they either deny or pursue the behavior those roles prescribe. Tartuffe, being an evil character, is destroyed when he is tricked into revealing his true nature. Oscar and Felix discover that, despite the friction occasioned by their being roommates, their true roles are those of friends. The two characters in *The Blood Knot* ultimately recognize that their only hope is to embrace their true roles as brothers as opposed to roles as racial antagonists. And Hamlet ultimately fulfills the nobility of his character, purging Denmark of its corruption.

Of course, Hamlet destroys himself in the process. But then drama frequently deals with the sobering truth that those attempting to live according to their highest ideals will almost inevitably find themselves in conflict with the established order of things. There are those cases in which the individual happily prevails (think of Jimmy Stewart's idealistic young senator in *Mr. Smith Goes to Washington*), but the truth at the heart of much tragedy is that the heroic challenging of the accepted order puts one at profound risk.

Much has been written about why one experiences a catharsis watching tragedy. How is it that witnessing the destruction of heroes produces in the audience not a profound depression but a kind of elation? My theory is that this feeling is a result of our knowledge that Hamlet, Antigone, Romeo and Juliet, and Iphigenia (to name but a few) ultimately embrace their true, higher natures. Polonius's advice, "To thine ownself be true" is an injunction few in real life have the courage to fully act upon, and there is something liberating about seeing characters who, in full knowledge of the frequently cataclysmic consequences, choose to be their truest selves. This is true not only of heroic characters but of such less-than-admirable figures as Medea and Macbeth. We may be horrified by their actions, but we can't deny that their actions ultimately are the fullest expression of their real constitutions.

What I find most useful about this formulation is that any script conceived embracing the roles-in-conflict principle necessarily has a multifaceted character at its center. Not a bad thing to have going for you when you sit down to write.

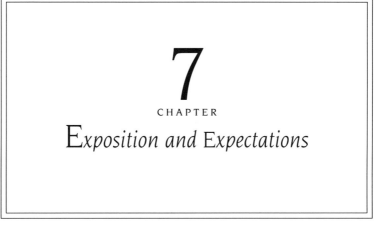

CHAPTER

Exposition and Expectations

NOT SO VERY LONG AGO, IT WAS COMMON PRACTICE TO START A play with a pair of secondary characters in a scene that ran along these lines:

MARY. Young Gregory was out late last night. He finally came back at three in the morning.
JOHN. Did he say anything about where he was or why there's such a big dent in his car?
MARY. No, but he'd had too much to drink, I can tell you that.
JOHN. I wonder if this has anything to do with the letter he received yesterday. The one that made him turn so pale.
MARY. I couldn't say. But this morning at breakfast you could have cut the tension between him and his parents with a knife.

All right, I'm exaggerating, but not by very much. The introductory conversation between two servants, or two gossips in the neighborhood, or a character newly returned from travels asking about events during his absence often kicked off the action. If you can call this action.

The idea behind such scenes was to pump the audience full of the information necessary to understand the subsequent events. Playgoers used to sit patiently for the first ten minutes or so knowing that enduring this sort of exposition was the price they had to pay in order to get to the good stuff. And I'm not talking only about plays by forgotten hacks. The only reason for the lame passage between Camillo and Archidamus in Act I, scene 1 of Shakespeare's *The Winter's Tale* is to help the audience get its bearings. (Just because Shakespeare is the best doesn't mean he didn't make his share of mistakes.)

Generally speaking, plays start faster than they used to. I think this is partially the result of television. Tune into a prime-time drama series, and you'll see something like this in the pre-credits action:

> *Stand-up comic onstage, telling jokes. Audience laughing. A woman in black carrying a purse slips in through the stage entrance. She moves to a door marked "Dressing Room," enters the room, and closes the door behind her. Inside, she switches on the light, looks around, sees sitting on the makeup table a framed photo of an attractive lady. Suddenly, she smashes the photo onto the floor so that the glass from the frame breaks. Onstage, the comic says goodnight and takes his bows. In a cheerful mood, he goes to his dressing room. He switches on the light, takes a step and hears a crunch. He looks down on the floor and sees he has stepped on the glass from the smashed frame. Then he hears a voice: "You were really cooking tonight, Charley. You were killing them." He turns and sees the woman standing behind the door, pointing a small pistol at him. Sweat builds on his upper lip. "And I always thought 'die laughing' was an expression," she says. Now she smiles. The camera pulls in on her finger on the trigger. Fade out. Bouncy music kicks in and the credits begin.*

Do you want to know who the woman is, why she smashed the picture, and whether she's going to ventilate Charley? You've got to stay tuned past the credits and the opening batch of commercials. If you do, you'll probably be willing to sit through some less immediately compelling stuff setting up other characters till the story returns to Charley and his mysterious visitor. And then odds are, having invested this much time, you'll stick around for the rest of the show. By beginning with a provocative but unexplained incident, the story has been launched, caught your attention, and given you enough reason to take the ride to the last stop.

The craft of writing for television has necessarily been affected by the nature of the audience's relation to the medium. Aware that the audience, holding channel changers in their hands, can switch to a competing program at any time, the writers know they have to serve up immediate and pressing reasons for viewers to stick around. Obviously, few are likely to stick around if the show starts with the equivalent of two servants relating offstage events. So a TV script tends to start with a scene that builds to a pressing dramatic question.

Of course, audiences don't come to the theater with channel changers in hand. But, after years of watching the box in their living rooms and getting used to the pacing of tales told there, they come to the theater in the habit of being plunged into the heart of the story quickly. To grab the playgoer fast, many contemporary playwrights have borrowed a page from television's book by beginning their plays with characters in the middle of high-energy sequences equivalent to the one introducing Charley's dilemma.

John Guare's remarkable play *Six Degrees of Separation* starts with two of the leading characters, Ouisa and Flan Kittredge, excitedly telling us in the audience about their narrow escape moments before from some unnamed threat, checking to see that none of their valuables have been stolen, savoring how close they may have come to death. Having established their hysteria, Guare then has them take us back several hours to a lower-key scene anticipating the arrival of a friend who is to join them for dinner. With the benefit of hindsight, we know that they will shortly be hyperventilating, so we watch carefully to see what part this dinner will play in the chain of events that leads to their alarums.

Guare could very well have *started* with the Kittredges discussing their dinner plans and then proceeded with the rest of the play as written. Doing this would not have meant omitting any of his story. But by kicking the piece off with the two in such an agitated state and then flashing back, Guare makes the audience sit up and take notice from the first moment. No coy wooing of the playgoer here; he snares our interest instantly. Knowing that the flashback holds the answer to the question, What's making the Kittredges so upset? the audience pays closer attention to the lower-key scene that follows than they would have if the play had started with that scene.

I'm not suggesting that all plays should begin in the middle of action, but quite a few would be improved if they did. I asked the members of a playwriting workshop I run to bring in scripts they were working on, and, as an experiment, we read excerpts from them, each time starting on page ten. In all but two cases, the writers decided their plays actually began better on their tenth page than on their first.

What about the information contained in the missing pages? My students discovered that most of it was implicit in the scenes we joined in progress. Instead of conscientiously setting up the circumstances for subsequent dramatic action, by beginning in the *middle* of dramatic action, the writers gave the audience the fun of figuring out the circumstances for themselves. Gone were the dull stretches of characters entering the stage, pouring drinks, and coyly doling out nuggets of self-introduction. Gone, too, were the one-way phone calls designed to sneak in exposition. Rather than switching on and warming up the scripts' motors and then coaxing them up to speed, the pieces began *in* speed. This gave them a sense of urgency from the word go, and that urgency made them compelling.

The opening of a play not only gets the story started, it also makes a contract with the audience. The first few minutes virtually announce, "This is the kind of play we're doing," and the audience sets its expectations accordingly. After all, we watch different genres with different expectations. If, say, we're watching a slice-of-life drama such as Frank D. Gilroy's *The Subject Was Roses*, at the very least we expect the Cleary family is not going to start floating around their Bronx apartment in defiance of Newton's laws of gravity. On the other hand, James M. Barrie swiftly makes certain that in *Peter Pan* we know we're in a world in which children may ignore Newton if they so choose.

It is very important, then, that the opening of your script set the audience's expectations correctly. If you break a promise to a friend in real life, you're liable to lose the trust and confidence of that friend. Break a promise to the people who have paid to see your play, they will respond with confusion and irritation, not reactions likely to help build good word-of-mouth. If you begin your play with a pair of bewigged fops trading quips in blank verse, you'd better not suddenly switch in the middle of the second act to a modern psychological thriller. Raising your curtain on a solo figure in black tights on a bare stage miming the life cycle would be a misleading introduction to a Neil Simon–style domestic comedy.

This may sound like very obvious advice, but some very savvy theatrical talents nearly lost a great musical because of such a miscalculation. A *Funny Thing Happened on the Way to the Forum* was trying out in a pre-Broadway engagement in Washington in 1962. According to all accounts, the show was substantially the one we've come to know, but the audiences weren't taking to it. The laughs were few and far between, and each night a dismaying chunk of the audience disappeared at intermission. The perplexed creative team—which included such celebrated figures as George Abbott, Larry Gelbart, Bert Shevelove, and Stephen Sondheim—asked director-choreographer Jerome Robbins to take a look and tell them where they were going wrong.

After the performance, Robbins informed them that the problem was with the opening number, a light-hearted little tune called "Love Is in the Air," which promised a romantic frolic. Instead of a romantic frolic, however, what followed was an evening of broad jokes, slapstick, and farcical intrigue. Robbins said what was needed was an opening that *promised* broad jokes, slapstick, and farcical intrigue. An opening, he insisted, should promise the audience what in fact the show to follow is going to deliver.

Composer-lyricist Stephen Sondheim went to his piano and wrote a song, entitled "Comedy Tonight," that did just that. According to legend, as soon as it was put in, the reaction to the show turned around completely. What had previously played to indifference now brought cheers. A *Funny Thing Happened* went on to New York where it received glowing reviews and was proclaimed a hit. It is now counted a classic musical comedy—all because the opening was changed.

Not only do you establish the genre of a show in the first few minutes, you also establish stylistic rights. Peter Shaffer's *Equus* begins with the image of a seventeen-year-old boy in a tableau with an actor wearing stylized hooves on his feet and a mask on his head. A light comes up on Dysart, a man we will soon learn is a psychiatrist. He tells us: "With one particular horse, called Nugget, he embraces." Instantly, by telling us we are to accept the masked and hoofed actor as a horse, Shaffer signals us that this play will employ metaphoric imagery. Also, by having Dysart address us at the top, he establishes that Dysart will serve as the play's narrator. We are now prepared for a stylized drama that will use flamboyant theatrical techniques to explore the theme of myth in modern life.

Similarly, at the top of *Six Degrees of Separation* Guare swiftly signals us that he reserves the right to (1) have any of his characters, at the drop of a hat and without self-consciousness, address the audience directly and (2) leap to any other time or place in the story with the briefest of transitions. And, indeed, throughout the script, both major and minor characters feel no compunction about making eye-contact with a theater full of playgoers and speaking their minds. What's more, scenes move abruptly back and forth in time and jump, without second thought, from the Kittredges' fancy apartment to Central Park to Greenwich Village and wherever else it is necessary to go to witness the essential events of the story. And, oh yes, the number of laughs at the show's beginning clearly indicates the audience is in for a comedy.

It is a truism among musical theater writers that the opening number is usually the last one you write because it is only after you've finished the rest of the show that you know what the opening should prepare the audience for. Straight plays are structurally less complicated than musicals, but upon completing a draft, a smart dramatist looks closely at the opening few pages to see if they correctly establish the world and style of the two hours to follow. The audience isn't likely to go through your door if you don't offer them the key to unlock it.

Even if you start your play in the middle of action, somehow you're still going to have to fill the people out front in on what they need to know in order to understand the significance of the events you present. So, we're back to that fearsome word, *exposition*.

Time out for a joke:

The scene is a banquet for stand-up comics. After dinner, the comics take turns getting up and telling stories. Except, because they all know all of the stories already, they don't have to actually *tell* the stories. All they have to do is tell the *numbers* of the stories in order to get appreciative laughter. So one old-timer gets up and says, "Twenty-three," and everybody falls apart. Then another gets up and says, "One hundred eight," and again the room explodes with laughter. Finally, a third, eager young comic gets up and says, "Sixty-two." Dead silence. He sits down embarrassed, muttering, "Damn, I never *could* tell that one right."

This joke is based on the concept of high-context communication. To explain what I mean by this, I must give you an incredibly superficial introduction to a gentleman named Edward T. Hall.

Hall is an anthropologist and the author of a series of books on the ways people communicate with each other aside from the literal meaning of the words they may use in conversation. In *The Silent Language*, he introduced the concept of body language—the degree to which we "read" others' gestures. In *The Hidden Dimension*, he dealt with some of the concepts underlying what I described earlier as negotiations over space. And, in one particularly useful section in his *Beyond Culture*, he describes what he terms high-context and low-context communications.

Low-context communication exists between people when there is a lack of shared knowledge, experience, or understanding, and this creates the need for the parties to explain a great deal to each other.

A tourist guide, for instance, has a low-context relationship with the people who take the tour. They don't know what the guide knows or else they wouldn't be paying to be shepherded around and provided with anecdotes and other nuggets of information relating to the sights. For that matter, *any* teaching situation is a low-context interaction—the teacher explicating a body of knowledge for the student. Whenever we consult a specialist, we similarly expect to be in a low-context relationship. If my doctor tells me that I'm suffering from some syndrome with a Latin name, I expect him to translate it into English and then share with me information regarding a suitable course of treatment.

On the other hand, high-context communication exists when the parties in question have a great deal of shared background in the area in which they are dealing. This enables them to interact in shorthand under the assumption that, employing a minimum of words and gestures, each is being understood by the other. The joke about the comics at the banquet rests upon the assumption that the comics have such high-context communication that merely saying a number will trigger a response to the story for which it stands.

Any interaction between people dealing in a field of shared expertise will be high-context. Two classical violinists talking together may refer to "the Bruch" and "the Mendelssohn," confident they are both discussing concerti by those composers. At a party, one lawyer may tell another lawyer about filing a motion for discovery, and the nonlawyers for the most part won't know what the hell those two are talking about. A couple of philosophers may wrangle over positive and negative concepts of liberty, and those not in the know won't recognize that these are terms Isaiah Berlin uses to differentiate the freedom *to* do something from the freedom *from* some limitation on the ability to do something. (Some philosophers get so high-context within their own schools that they can't even talk high-context with philosophers from other schools.) Basically, then, people who have a high-context relationship are those who are in the know about the subject they're discussing.

Of course, people may have a high-context relationship relating to one area and not another. For instance, a brain surgeon from Chicago will have a high-context relationship with a brain surgeon from San Diego regarding the topic of brain surgery, but if the Chicagoan makes a reference to Ann Sather's, the surgeon from San Diego, not being familiar with Chicago, may not recognize this as a well-known restaurant on Belmont specializing in Swedish cooking. But the Chicago brain surgeon mentioning Ann Sather's may very well elicit, "Those meatballs are terrific!" from a guard for the Chicago Bears.

Obviously this does not just apply to professions. A friend who was around when I was in the middle of a disastrous relationship with a lady named Patricia will know why I wince when

I hear that name, whereas a friend I've met since Patricia disappeared from my life and who has not heard my tale of woe won't understand why I excuse myself to daub my eyes.

Right now, most comics assume a high-context relationship with their audience when it comes to TV. The late Gilda Radner's character, Bawbwa Wawa, may make a contemporary audience howl, but odds are an audience fifty years from now won't be familiar with Barbara Walters and won't have the slightest idea of why the audience is laughing. But then Aristophanes's plays are full of high-context jokes we can't understand because we don't share the references that he rightly assumed his audience would appreciate. We sit through some passages of Shakespeare very solemnly, not having sufficient familiarity with Elizabethan slang to know he's reeling off some great dirty jokes.

A quick way to differentiate between high-context and low-context communication may be to say that high-context communication relies mostly on the implicit and low-context requires explicitness.

Now, what does all this have to do with playwriting?

When high-context dialogue or behavior occurs between characters onstage, the audience infers a high degree of familiarity between the characters. When low-context dialogue or behavior occurs, the audience infers a lack of familiarity between the characters. So: *the context level of the dialogue should match the context level of the relationship being portrayed.*

Easier said that done. In the workshops I teach, hardly a session goes by when a student doesn't bring in a scene in which people who have been in each other's lives for years talk to each other endlessly about things they already know.

Not that this sort of thing is limited to students. Here's a taste of Ibsen's *The Master Builder* with Solness and Dr. Herdal:

DR. HERDAL. Yes, I must say it seems to me you have had the luck
  on your side to an astounding degree.
SOLNESS (*suppressing a gloomy smile*). So I have, I can't complain on
  that account.
DR. HERDAL. To begin with, that grim robbers' roost was burnt down
  for you. And that was certainly a fortunate thing.

SOLNESS. Don't forget—it was the home of Aline's family.

DR. HERDAL. Yes, it must have caused her great distress.

SOLNESS. She has not recovered yet—not in all these twelve or thirteen years.

DR. HERDAL. Ah, but what happened then must have been the worst blow for her.

SOLNESS. The one thing with the other.

DR. HERDAL. But you—you built upon the ruins. You began as a poor boy from a country village—and now you are at the head of your profession. Ah, yes, Mr. Solness, you have certainly had fortune on your side.

The grinding you hear in the background is my teeth. This sort of thing drives me crazy. Here you have two men who have known each other for a long time, yet they rehearse Solness's life in such detail that it undermines our belief that they've known each other so much as ten minutes. Here we have what Ibsen expects us to believe is a relatively high context relationship between a man and his doctor of many years, yet they speak low-context dialogue when it comes to matters with which they are both intimately familiar. Obviously, the only reason they are talking like this is for the audience to overhear exposition. But the trick of good naturalistic exposition is to make it not *sound* like exposition. This chunk all but takes out an advertisement as to its function.

Even some fine contemporary playwrights make this mistake. The entire first act of Athol Fugard's A *Lesson from Aloes* is exposition thrown at each other by a couple who have been married for a long time and, in fact, for months have been limited to nobody *but* each other for conversation, which makes it all the more jarring that these two discuss such familiar topics in the exhaustive detail that they do. The irony is that almost all of what they are required by the author to convey to the audience so laboriously is implicit in Fugard's marvelous second act. With only minor changes, I think the second act by itself could stand more effectively as a complete play.

Offhand I can't think of an example of the opposite—a playwright erring by having characters in a low-context relationship speak inappropriately high-context dialogue. There are, however, examples of characters tripping themselves up by accidentally revealing they have information they should not know. In *The Godfather, Part* II, it is just such a slip that makes Michael (played by Al Pacino) realize that he has been betrayed by his brother Fredo (John Cazale). A lot of crime stories are resolved by having a character make such a slip, mentioning some detail to which only the culprit could have access. (See the end of David Mamet's *Glengarry Glen Ross* when Shelley Levene inadvertently implicates himself in the burglary of the sales office.)

If a writer goes astray with the context level of his or her dialogue, it's usually in the process of trying to cram in some exposition, as in the Ibsen and Fugard examples. This is understandable from a tactical point of view. As I said, low-context communication usually involves explanation, so the writer, having a low-context relationship with the audience regarding the past histories and circumstances of his characters, has the natural impulse to use a low-context mode. But, understandable or not, you have to be careful not to let your low-context relationship with the audience lead you to write low-context dialogue for characters who have a high-context relationship.

It is relatively easy to write exposition when you have characters in a low-context situation. This is one of the reasons why the first episodes of TV series frequently are concerned with a character entering a new milieu. As Lou Grant arrived at the newspaper that was to be his home for several seasons, he was introduced to the characters who would become the regulars on the series. (Similarly, the first episode of the *Mary Tyler Moore Show* dealt with Mary's first day in that Minneapolis newsroom — during which, of course, she and we first met Lou, among others.)

The character who arrives in a new milieu at the beginning of a piece has a natural motivation for finding out who's who and what's what. As he or she asks pertinent questions, we in the audience absorb the information at the same time. You will recall that in Chapter 5, I described how Peter Stone used a delegate named Lymon Hall to create an occasion for introducing the rest of the delegates to the Continental Congress. This scene, a marvelous example of low-context exposition, is predicated on Hall being new to the Congress and so needing to be acclimated. Other examples:

The King and I begins with Anna and her son, Louis, arriving in Siam, a country about whose customs they know very little. As they have the ropes explained to them (e.g., the bit about not having one's head higher than the king's), we learn them too. But, because Anna and Louis have an organic reason to find all of this stuff out, and the people they encounter have organic reasons to tell them, the exposition doesn't feel awkward.

In Herb Gardner's A *Thousand Clowns*, when Sandy meets Murray, she is gathering data for the case to which she's assigned, so, again, she has a logical reason to ask all sorts of questions during the course of which we learn all we need to know about the circumstances of Murray's "adoption" of his nephew.

In D. L. Coburn's *The Gin Game*, the play begins with our understanding that Fonsia is new to the rest home, so Weller can explain a lot about the place as well as introduce himself to her (and to us).

In *Streetcar*, Blanche's arrival at Stanley and Stella's apartment logically prompts Stella to explain certain things about how life is lived on this alien territory. Blanche and Stanley, never having met each other before, are also given license to probe and find out things about each other as we out front take it all in. There is also a very detailed "getting-to-know-you" scene between Blanche and Mitch, which reveals much of both of their backgrounds and history without straining credibility.

Sometimes, a playwright brings in a secondary character *specifically* to bring out background information. For example: the first scene with the telephone man in Neil Simon's *Barefoot in the Park*. Amusing as he is, in truth he contributes nothing to the forward motion of the plot. He is there to perform a task, and Simon uses him to give Corie an opportunity to tell someone about her situation.

There are certain events that require low-context material as part of their form and so may be usefully invoked in a script as a way of getting exposition out. Some examples include job interviews (almost all of A *Chorus Line* is low-context exposition within the framework of an audition); the aftermath of medical checkups (see Kurosawa's film *Ikuru*); and instructional situations (see William Gibson's *The Miracle Worker*).

And trials. Trials are expositional by their very nature. The object of examination and cross-examination is to convey information to the jury. Each witness is introduced by full name; the lawyers elicit details of his or her occupation, credentials, residence, and so on; and then we observe a battery of questions of specific relevance to the dramatic meat of the play. ("Let me get this straight, Dr. Frobisher. You're saying that because the victim's dinner was undigested, he couldn't have been shot much past mealtime?")

In Greek tragedies, frequently the chorus was assigned the job of cluing the audience in on the relevant details. No pretense of naturalism here, just a bunch of people taking the license to address us directly and say, in essence, "OK, here's what you need to know." Shakespeare occasionally indulged in this technique, most famously with the introduction and transitional passages in *Henry V*. Brecht frequently didn't want to be bothered getting the facts out subtly; actors in his plays often hold up signs or simply turn to the audience and announce what must be known in order to understand the scene that follows.

An analogous technique appears in some musicals, particularly in chorus numbers. For instance, there is no logically motivated reason for all of the citizens of River City to line up facing downstage and explicitly describe their own ethos in "Iowa Stubborn." Similarly, the crowd dressed in Oliver Smith clothes at the racetrack sing things in the "Ascot Gavotte" Alan Jay Lerner could not have gotten away with having them say.

But in naturalistic drama it isn't stylistically appropriate to have things explicitly explained to the audience, and sometimes you will find yourself dealing with characters who, because they know each other very well, cannot logically have low-context exposition shoved into their mouths.

Which brings us to the question: How *does* one deal with exposition when the characters start off in a high-context relationship?

I think the answer is to depict a negotiation between the characters that would exist only *given* the material you wish to expose. Early in Neil Simon's *The Sunshine Boys*, for instance, there is a scene between an old man named Willie and his nephew Ben. Willie asks Ben why he didn't get sent out to auditions for two musicals that have just begun rehearsing.

BEN. Because there were no parts for you. One of them is a young
    rock musical and the other show is all black.
WILLIE. What's the matter, I can't do black? I did black in 1928. And
    when I did black, you understood the words, not like today.

Simon's intention is to let us know that Willie used to perform in vaudeville and in musicals. Instead of having Willie say so directly, he sets up a conflict between Willie and his nephew, who also happens to be an agent. Willie complains about not having gotten an audition for the two musicals. Out front, we reason that only a performer would complain about not having had the chance to audition. Willie talks about having played in blackface, and the audience, knowing how long it has been since it was socially acceptable for white actors to play in blackface, can figure out how far back Willie's career began. That's a lot of information conveyed entertainingly in a handful of lines.

David Mamet is a master of high-context exposition. Look at the first scene of *Glengarry Glen Ross*. Sitting in a booth in a Chinese restaurant, a nervous man named Shelly Levene tries to bribe another man named Williamson to give him some choice leads. As they negotiate over the leads—how much Levene will pay, when he will pay, and so forth—we begin to realize that Levene is a real estate salesman in trouble and that Williamson is the office manager who controls which salesmen have access to which opportunities to make a sale. We also learn about the competition between the salesmen—the winners get prizes, the losers get fired—and that Levene is currently way behind.

The wonder of this scene is that we learn all of this indirectly. All of our understanding of Levene's situation and the competition is the by-product of his attempt to beg, wheedle, charm, or bully Williamson into giving him a crack at the list of potential customers most likely to result in a sale. The ostensible subject of the scene is the attempted bribe, but the result is that, by the end, we have a pretty thorough understanding of the internal politics of the company that employs both men.

If this reminds you of my earlier theories on negotiations over objects and the use of premises and conclusions, good. All of these ideas apply here. Levene and Williamson are indeed negotiating over something—the leads. Our understanding of the nature of their relationship is revealed through the way they deal with each other. And, because of what they negotiate over and how, we come to conclusions about the larger picture around them.

Edward Albee's *Who's Afraid of Virginia Woolf?* offers expert writing of both high- and low-context exposition: The first several pages introduce us to George and Martha returning to their home late at night. He claims to be too tired to be helpful when she tries to remember the name of a Bette Davis movie. She says she doesn't know why he's so tired: "[Y]ou haven't *done* anything all day; you didn't have any classes or anything. . . . " He gripes about "these goddamn Saturday night orgies" her father sets up. She complains about his moping around the party; he complains about her raucousness at the party. She upsets his assumption that they're about to turn in for the night by telling him they have guests. "You met them tonight . . . they're new . . . he's in the math department, or something." When George protests the lateness of the hour, she tells him that "Daddy said we should be nice to them."

There is a good deal more to the scene, but what I've described above should be enough to set up certain inferences. One is that George and Martha are married and have a rather fractious relationship, Martha inclined to shoot her mouth off, and George inclined to mostly duck and cover. It is also reasonable to assume that they live in an academic environment—probably a college ("you didn't have any classes or anything" and "he's in the math department"). Additionally, from the fact that her father sets up parties to which faculty members are summoned, and that "Daddy" can issue an injunction that they "should be nice to" the new couple, one gathers that George's father-in-law is a high-muck-a-muck in the college hierarchy.

As George and Martha have been married for years and know each other backwards and forwards, it would have been unbelievable if Albee had had them detail to each other the circumstances of their lives. So Albee has introduced them wrangling over matters that they would only discuss *given* the fact that they are married and that George is on the faculty of a college where Martha's father is a bigwig. Though none of their circumstances is explicitly stated, Albee's scene is so crafted that, through implication, it clearly conveys the necessary information to anyone who is halfway conscious.

Shortly after, Nick and Honey enter. Being new to the campus and knowing little more about George and Martha than their names, Nick and Honey are in a low-context relationship to the older couple. This gives Albee an organic reason for George and Martha to tell a good deal about themselves and Nick and Honey to respond in kind. Establishing the two couples as being in a low-context relationship, Albee has the license to have them speak to each other in a low-context mode. The play would have been substantially different if, instead of being new to the campus, Nick and Honey had been established by Albee as having been there for the past year or so. (If they had, Nick and Honey probably would have been smart enough to forgo the opportunity to visit George and Martha!)

To summarize, because George and Martha have a high-context relationship, Albee has written their initial scene employing high-context dialogue. Because Nick and Honey have a low-context relationship with George and Martha, Albee has justification for writing the interactions between the newly acquainted couple employing low-context dialogue.

Writing high-context exposition requires logical thinking. You have to work backward. You have to know what circumstances you want the audience to understand, then you have to construct a scene that could only be played given those circumstances. Say I want to get across the fact that the widowed mother of two sisters has died recently. Rather than having the sisters explain endlessly what they both already know—that Mom is dead—I might have them argue over which of them is going to end up with Mom's piano. Out front, the audience will figure that they wouldn't be fighting over the piano if Mom were still around to play it herself.

Or say I want to reveal that Uncle Omar is serving a prison sentence. I might write a scene in which his nephew, about to visit him, is entrusted with gifts or notes by other members of the family. "No point in sending those power tools with me. The guards won't let me give them to him." The word "guards" will tip the audience off to the idea of Omar's being incarcerated, without me having to type the word prison.

OK, the theoretical idea is simple. Doing it, though, is hard. In fact, I think that writing high-context exposition is among the most difficult technical tasks of playwriting. As with any technical task, mastery will come only with observation and practice.

So, as you're watching shows or reading scripts, analyze which context level the early scenes play on. If it's low-context, ask yourself what about the set-up allows the characters to explain things to each other without sounding as if they're Mickey Mousing. If it's high-context, figure out how the manifest negotiation conveys by implication the information the writer is trying to convey.

8

CHAPTER

Dialogue

THOUGH I'VE MADE THE POINT THAT THE ESSENCE OF A PLAY IS not so much what the characters say as what they do (what they say being only one aspect of what they do), most of the text of a script is made up of what they say: the dialogue.

In earlier chapters, I've demonstrated how employing such concepts as premises and conclusions, negotiations, and high- and low-context exposition influences the way characters speak. In this chapter, I want to address other considerations.

When I introduced the subject of roles in conflict, I said that each of us speaks with not one voice, but with a repertory of voices, and that each of these voices represents one of our roles. So it is with characters. Before writing dialogue, you have to ascertain which roles the characters in the scene will play with each other. This, in turn, determines which voices they will use in speaking with each other.

> We have rules, Fergus. The rules are meant to be obeyed, partic- ularly with respect to works of art donated to this institution by alumni. If you aspire to someday become an alumnus yourself, you will conform to these rules. And you will kindly stop smirk- ing while I address you.

The speaker—the principal of a private school talking to a student caught vandalizing.

> The statue? No, no, please, don't worry about that. If the groundskeeper can't get the paint off, I'll just have him paint white over it. I understand about high spirits. I was young once

myself, you know. Only, in the future, if you could, uh, direct these high spirits in a less public manner?

The same principal upon discovering that the student is the son of a family thinking of donating twenty million dollars to the school.

The same principal talking to the same student, different voices. The first voice, formal and imperious; the second, informal and avuncular.

So a character's speech is very much dependent on what that character believes is his or her *status* in relation to the other person or persons in the scene. In the first example, under the impression that he is addressing "just" a student, the principal is employing an officious voice to reinforce his superior position. In the second example, aware that the way he treats the student may affect his school's fortunes, the principal is toning down the harshness and, while attempting to maintain a nominally superior position, trying to curry favor.

In addition to the relative statuses of the characters in the scene, obviously you have to give some thought to making certain their dialogue accurately reflects the amount of schooling they have had. You're not going to win many points in the credibility sweepstakes if you have an English professor say, "Between you and I," in polite conversation. However, this ungrammatical phrase would be perfectly consistent with the character of Adelaide in *Guys and Dolls*.

Stephen Sondheim learned this lesson during the previews of *West Side Story*. In a talk to the Dramatists Guild, he recalled his friend, lyricist Sheldon Harnick, gently suggesting that there was a problem with Sondheim's lyric for "I Feel Pretty." The song is supposed to express the perspective of an uneducated Puerto Rican girl, but the internal rhymes Sondheim had her sing made her someone (as he put it) who "would not have been unwelcome in Noel Coward's living room." (Sondheim tried to substitute a revised lyric, but his collaborators wouldn't allow the change.)

Other experience besides education has an impact on what one says and how one says it. In *Pygmalion*, George Bernard

Shaw has Henry Higgins claim that on the basis of someone's speech, "I can place any man within six miles. I can place him within two miles in London. Sometimes within two streets."

The members of the audience may not have ears as acute as Higgins's, but they'll certainly notice glaring inconsistencies between where the characters claim to hail from and the way they talk. You wouldn't believe an inner-city American telling someone to "Sod off," while it might be just the thing for an inner-city Londoner. Despite the leveling impact of television, there are still readily identifiable accents and idioms specific to southerners, westerners, and easterners. If the regional origins of your characters are important, then it behooves you to do the research to find out what expressions and verbal tics are associated with which regions. If you're going to include a character from Toronto, for instance, it's useful to know that many natives of that city have the habit of appending "eh?" to the ends of their sentences. If you're going to set your story in a town near the Mexican border, you're probably going to need some familiarity with Spanglish, that ad hoc mixture of Spanish and English that has developed because of the intermingling of the cultures.

Oral histories and collections of interviews are particularly useful for researching the impact of status, education, and experience on the way people talk. Studs Terkel has published a series of books featuring edited transcripts of conversations with a wide array of people. Aside from the fascinating range of experiences and opinions he has recorded, these volumes are treasure troves of linguistic sampling. His book *Race* demonstrates some of the differences in the way blacks and whites use the language. His *Division Street* juxtaposes the usage of different classes. *The Good War* offers access to references and expressions from World War II.

Other authors have also captured in a distilled form the varieties of human communication. During the Depression, the Works Progress Administration employed writers to interview a broad range of Americans; *First Person America*, edited by Ann Banks, presents a generous sampling of these interviews and should be required reading for anyone attempting to portray that era. Joseph Kisseloff's *You Must Remember This* records and contrasts the speech of more than fifty years of Manhattanites of varied backgrounds. Donald Honig has produced a series of books—among them, *Baseball When the Grass Was Real* and *Baseball Between the Lines*—full of vivid and colorful interviews with ball players of the past.

The books mentioned above mostly deal with noncelebrity subjects. For a taste of how the privileged, talented, and famous speak, several periodicals—among them, *Newsday*, *Playboy*, *Interview*, and *Omni*—offer interviews in a question-and-answer form. I am also fond of Bill Moyers's *World of Ideas* volumes, which feature dozens of intellectuals, from various disciplines, in conversation.

In addition, official sources such as court transcripts and the *Congressional Record* may be invaluable. When researching *American Enterprise*, a play that depicts a labor struggle in the Chicago of the late 1800s, I was pleased to discover that most of the principle figures in my cast of characters had testified in front of the Federal Strike Commission of 1893. At the Library of Congress, I found page after page of my characters being questioned at length on some of the very events I was portraying. Aside from historical details I gleaned from this testimony, I also became familiar with the speech patterns and logic of the figures I was attempting to bring to life. (In fact, I built one extended scene out of an edited version of the appearance of my protagonist in front of the hostile members of the Commission.)

As useful as referring to preexistent texts is, I cannot overestimate the value of taking out a cassette machine, recording conversations, and transcribing them yourself. If you are shy about taping your friends, then as an exercise try taping and transcribing an episode of a TV talk show such as *Phil Donahue* or *Oprah Winfrey*. If you listen to and type—word for word—this spontaneous, "real life" speech, you will make a number of discoveries. Among them: how often people interrupt themselves and each other, either to correct word choices or to pursue a new idea that has just occurred to them; how often people digress in the middle of making their points; and how few adjectives people tend to use in conversation.

Tim Kazurinsky, who was a regular on *Saturday Night Live* for a few seasons, told me a story that underscores this last point. During rehearsal, a hot-tempered guest star, who shall remain nameless, exploded at the writers, "Don't give me so many fucking adjectives! I'm the actor! I supply the fucking adjectives!" While intemperately phrased (and adorned with his adjective of choice), there is wisdom in this outburst. You don't need a character to say, "I'm desperately tired." If the actor is any good at all, the condition of being desperately tired will be conveyed through the way he or she says, "Anybody see my *National Geographic*?" In fact, if you listen to actors working on a scene that has some claim to naturalism, you'll find it's common for them to hesitate a hair before saying a high-octane adjective or adverb. This always brings to my mind the image of a stunt driver backing up to gain speed so as to leap a chasm. Actors, particularly American actors, feel faintly embarrassed by rich language, and they take that little pause so as to give the appearance that their characters are working to come up with the word in question. (We tend to do this ourselves on the infrequent occasions when we use such words in conversation.)

In fact, I find that there is no clearer tip-off that a writer is new to playwriting than to encounter a lot of adjectives and adverbs in the dialogue.

Keeping adjectives and adverbs to a believable minimum doesn't doom your language to blandness.

In preparing the case against crime boss John Gotti, the federal government tapped his line. The results of that tap were entered into the public record and published. Here's a verbatim excerpt in which Gotti talks about his attitude towards his lawyers:

> If you win the case, hey, I win the case, I know I gotta do the right thing by you. You win, I promise you fifty—you get seventy-five! You get a fuckin' bonus, fifty percent, because we're here now. Now we go up the corner, hustle a buck. Man, you, you just got me a hundred fifty years. You want to leave my son destitute and my family destitute. What the fuck is it all about? Was it you that put me on this earth to rob and make you rich and me poor? Go fuck yourself!

If you analyze the parts of speech in this passage, you'll find very few adjectives or adverbs, the sole "fancy" one being *destitute*. Yet I don't think it can be denied that this is a prime example of colorful and idiomatic American speech.

Some years ago, I got together with a pair of friends named Stephen Johnson and Sandra Hastie to try a small experiment in using improvisation in writing. I brought to one of our sessions a brief outline of a scene:

Frank is expecting his friends, a married couple named Marty and Diane, to stop by his office and pick him up for an evening out together. Marty arrives before Diane. He has a little request: He would like Frank to confirm to his wife that he spent the previous evening with Frank. Frank, upset that Marty wants to use him to supply an alibi for what becomes apparent has been an infidelity, refuses. Marty argues but finally accepts Frank's refusal. Or says he does. When Diane does show up and does indeed raise the subject of Marty's whereabouts the evening before, Marty tells his lie. Boxed into a corner, Frank confirms it, but with an awkwardness that makes Diane suspect the truth. At the scene's end, it is apparent the marriage and the friendships are in jeopardy.

Stephen, Sandra, and I sat around a cassette recorder and improvised our way through this scene three times. I then transcribed the three versions. I edited what I thought were the most effective passages and wrote some new material until I had the final piece, a short play called *Cover* (which is published in the Samuel French anthology, 25 *Ten-Minute Plays from Actors Theatre of Louisville*). Here is an excerpt:

MARTY. There's a favor I want to ask of you.
FRANK. Ask away.
MARTY. OK. Well, see, as a topic of conversation, it may come up
    during the evening where I was last night. And it would make it a
    lot easier if we could decide between us that I was with you.
FRANK. To say that?

MARTY. Not to say necessarily, but to sort of give the impression that we were together. It would make things a lot simpler for me. I mean, if it comes up.

FRANK. You want me to say—

MARTY. Just to say—

FRANK. That you and I—

MARTY. That we were—

FRANK. Together—

MARTY. Together—

FRANK. Last night.

MARTY. Yeah.

FRANK. You want me to lie.

MARTY. Well . . .

FRANK. Not "well." You want me to lie.

MARTY. Well . . .

FRANK. That's what you're asking.

MARTY. I wouldn't put it—

FRANK. Is that what you're asking?

MARTY. Well, yes.

FRANK. To lie?

MARTY. A little bit. Just to give the impression so that Diane won't worry. To avoid confusion and upset for her.

FRANK. I see. You want me to do a favor for you for her.

MARTY. I couldn't have said it better myself.

FRANK. Where *were* you last night? I mean, I have to know.

MARTY. It doesn't matter.

FRANK. Well, yes, it does. I have to know whether you're wanting me to tell a white lie or a black lie.

MARTY. It's a white lie.

FRANK. How white? I mean, where were you?

MARTY. I was out.

FRANK. Alone? With someone?

MARTY. With someone.

FRANK. Yeah?

MARTY. Diane wouldn't understand.

FRANK. A woman?

MARTY. She'd take it the wrong way.

FRANK. You were out with another woman.

MARTY. Yes, I was out with another woman.

FRANK. I see. And that's a white lie?

MARTY. It's no big deal.

FRANK. I'm sorry, I can't do it.

MARTY. Hey, really, it's no big deal.

FRANK. No, I wouldn't feel good about it.

MARTY. Why not? It's just a little favor.

FRANK. It's not a little . . . you're asking me to lie to her. You don't understand. She's my friend.

MARTY. Aren't I your friend?

FRANK. You're my friend and she's my friend. But she's not my friend because you're my friend. I mean, it's not that you and I have a primary friendship and she's a secondary friend by extension. You're both primary friends.

MARTY. I understand that.

FRANK. You don't break that trust.

MARTY. I'm not asking you to break that trust. I'm asking you to spare her confusion and upset.

FRANK. You're asking me to lie to her.

MARTY. To give a different impression of the truth.

FRANK. A false impression, which is a lie.

MARTY. You've never told a lie in your life?

FRANK. That's not the issue.

MARTY. Of course it's the issue. You're saying you don't tell lies.

FRANK. I'm saying I will not tell *this* lie.

MARTY. How do you decide when you will or will not tell a lie?

FRANK. I try not to lie.

MARTY. But what makes you decide if you'll tell a given lie? Say that an opportunity for a lie presents itself—how do you decide if you'll tell it?

FRANK. This is not the issue.

MARTY. You have told lies, haven't you? You've told lies in the past.

FRANK. I have, but that has nothing to do with this.

MARTY. You just won't tell a lie for me.

I quote this excerpt to introduce the concept of the trigger word or phrase.

If you look closely at the passage above, you'll see that most of the lines are triggered by words or phrases in the lines immediately preceding. For instance:

FRANK. You're asking me to lie to her.

This moves Marty to contradict the characterization of his request. "To lie to her" triggers the impulse to rephrase as follows:

MARTY. To give a different impression of the truth.

Now it's Frank's turn to contradict Marty's characterization, to challenge the words "a different impression" by responding:

FRANK. A false impression, which is a lie.

Marty, picking up the word "lie," uses it for the basis of his next line to Frank:

MARTY. You've never told a lie in your life?

Frank objects to the introduction of this topic:

FRANK. That's not the issue.

Marty directly contradicts the question of relevance, modifying Frank's line:

MARTY. Of course it's the issue. You're saying you don't tell lies.

And now Frank modifies Marty's most recent line in his reply:

FRANK. I'm saying I will not tell *this* lie.

In each case, there is a hot word or phrase or idea that compels the other character to respond—to object, challenge, or modify what the other person has said. I believe the fact that this material originated in actors' improvisation, rather than the mind of a single writer, accounts for the degree to which this pattern of trigger and response appears in this scene.

Usually actors create behavior to justify the text they are given. For instance, an actress cast as Martha in *Who's Afraid of Virginia Woolf?* looks at Albee's script with the task of finding things to do on the stage that will support her saying those words. In such situations, actors have to work backwards, searching in rehearsal for ways to create the illusion that their lines are the spontaneous extension of the pursuit of their goals.

Improvisational actors find themselves in a position closer to the position in which we find ourselves in daily life. Except in those rare situations in which a lot is at stake depending on the specific words we use, in normal conversation we really don't *think* very much about the phrasing of most of what we say. We keep our attention fixed on what we hope to achieve and trust that when we open our mouths, words will be there. And they are. In fact, sometimes they tumble out at an astonishing rate. And sometimes, in the tumbling, we say more than we intended.

In ways similar to our daily encounters, actors improvising a scene place less emphasis on language and more on the logistics their characters employ in the pursuit of their goals. The dialogue they come up with is, by definition, speakable because it has come into being *as speech*.

The task of dramatists attempting to write naturalistic dialogue at their keyboards is to come up with text that gives the illusion of originating spontaneously in the mouths of their characters. Dramatists who have had experience in or a good deal of exposure to improvisation have a special advantage because they are more conscious of this concept of dialogue as an extension of trying to achieve objectives. David Mamet, who has established a particular reputation for colloquial American speech, absorbed a good deal from the actors at Second City while he was a busboy there. He also attended workshops run by Second City director Del Close, and he worked some as an actor under Close's direction. Lanford Wilson told me that during the year he attended the University of Chicago, he also spent a lot of time at Second City and that much of the way he approaches dialogue has been influenced by watching the actors there improvise. And the list of improvisational alumni who have distinguished themselves writing for film, TV, and the stage would run into the scores. One of the key elements that characterizes much of their writing is this trigger principle.

The excerpt I quoted from *Cover* illustrates this principle in a particularly intense form—a heated discussion. But the trigger principle also comes into play in exchanges not based in confrontation and challenge. It may indeed be a confirmation of what the other person has said ("Yes! Yes!"), or it may be some new image, idea, or concern that has been brought to mind because of what the other person said.

LORRAINE. I thought I'd get the same kind of computer that Gina has.
PAT. Oh, Gina!
LORRAINE. What?
PAT. I just remembered—she left a message for me yesterday and I haven't called her back.

I'm not claiming that these are brilliant exchanges, but they are believable. Instead of sounding as if they were written, they have some of the flavor of two independent minds interacting and provoking thoughts from each other.

"I Remember It Well," one of Lerner and Loewe's most charming songs for *Gigi*, illustrates the principle at work in a musical. Honore is remembering an affair he had years ago with Grandmama. As he rhapsodizes over the particulars of their courtship, it becomes apparent that he has gotten almost all of the details wrong. By my count, Honore remembers twelve specifics—among them, when he and Grandmama met, with whom they dined, the range of the singer in the restaurant, the nationality of the songs, what Grandmama wore, what belonging she lost that night—and every specific prompts a correction from Grandmama, until it becomes apparent that the only thing Honore has remembered correctly is the fact of their romance. In fact, virtually the entire lyric is based on the trigger principle.

It is very important not to allow a speech to go on too far past its most provocative line before another character responds.

DETECTIVE SHUMSKY. I arrested your daughter's fourth-grade teacher yesterday for aggravated assault and indecent exposure. Then I went to Bernice's Pancake Palace and had the best strawberry pancakes I've ever had. You ever had their strawberry pancakes? Lots of whipped cream and mounds of strawberries in syrup? I could feel my belt getting smaller.
NAOMI. Indecent exposure?!

The actress playing Naomi undoubtedly would feel the impulse to say "Indecent exposure?!" before Detective Shumsky had much opportunity to launch into his ode to strawberry pancakes, but, because the playwright has delayed the natural response, the actress would be stuck trying to come up with reasons to justify the delay. I doubt that she would thank the playwright for putting her into this uncomfortable situation.

I also want to make the point that characters are character-ized not only by what they say or do, but by what others say or do *in reference to them*. In Hecht and MacArthur's three-act play, *The Front Page*, Walter Burns doesn't make his entrance until the end of the second act. Yet we have a very clear understanding of who he is before we lay eyes on him. We have heard the motley group of hard-bitten reporters talk about him with a mixture of awe and fear, and we have seen Hildy Johnson argue with him on the phone, so we are thoroughly prepared for the cheerful bully who hijacks the stage when he bursts onto the scene.

Again, an insight from improvisational theater comes to mind. One of the exercises involves Player A leaving the room while Players B and C decide, between them, who they are and who A is. Player A then returns to the room, without being told any of this. Players B and C begin an improvised scene, and Player A is supposed to figure out who he or she is entirely through the way that Players B and C behave and involve her or him in the action.

In the following, Players A and B are women, and Player C is a man.

B. I don't know what the point of this is.

C. Honey, you agreed.

B. Fine, I agreed. But we've been to so many people, and paid all this money, and still you don't pick up your socks—

C. Oh, God, here we go with the socks again—

B. The socks are a big part of it. The fact that you don't think enough of me to—

C. All right, all right.

B (*to* A). I happen to think that this speaks to, you know, his attitude about me. If he had respect for me instead of thinking of me as his own personal maid—

C. That's not how I think of you—

B (*to* A). Do *you* think I'm crazy?

By this time, Player A has almost certainly figured out she is a marriage counselor. Notice that nobody has explicitly *called* her a marriage counselor, but the manner in which Players B and C have behaved in front of her makes the conclusion inevitable.

In this case, Player A's profession has been established without the actress saying anything. But more can be established than profession. Let's go back to the school principal I introduced at the beginning of this chapter.

> We have rules, Fergus. The rules are meant to be obeyed, particularly with respect to works of art donated to this institution by alumni. If you aspire to someday become an alumnus yourself, you will conform to these rules. And you will kindly stop smirking while I address you.

At the same time the audience is becoming directly familiar with the principal, it is coming to some conclusions about the person he is addressing. We know that he is a student named Fergus. We know that he is a vandal. And, if we can trust the principal's characterization of the expression on the student's face, we know that Fergus has an insolent manner.

A basic principle of psychology holds that to a substantial degree we see ourselves in the mirrors of the eyes of the people around us. If, whenever I walk down the street, people make some effort to keep from getting too close to me, I'm going to think of myself as a repellent creature. If, on the other hand, people constantly approach me and overwhelm me with praise, I'm going to think I'm pretty hot stuff.Carrying this principle to the stage, if every character in your script speaks to Mr. Jones in an obsequious manner, Mr. Jones, without saying anything, will be established as someone with power over the others.

The bottom line is that composing credible and dynamic dialogue requires dramatists to have a thorough understanding of the people into whose mouths they are putting words. How characters talk to each other is influenced by the nature of what they want from each other, their relative statuses, and their educational, ethnic, and regional backgrounds (as well as such other elements as their temperaments and their physical conditions). Phrased like this, the task may sound daunting, but take comfort in the fact that you already know a good deal about dialogue just by virtue of inventing so much of it for yourself everyday.

9

CHAPTER

Violating Rituals

IN CHAPTER 4 I WROTE ABOUT EVENT STRUCTURE AND HOW invoking an event can trigger the audience's expectations regarding the shape of a play or a scene. In this chapter, we'll explore what happens if, after invoking the event, you violate those expectations.

Mad Magazine once ran a parody of *Who's Afraid of Virginia Woolf?* As you probably remember, the secret of the play is that the son to whom George and Martha keep referring (and whom George metaphorically kills toward the end) is imaginary; the couple are incapable of having children. The revelation of this secret packs considerable dramatic punch and goes a long way towards helping the audience understand the dynamics of the marriage. The *Mad* parody, too, depicted George and Martha quarreling bitterly about their son. This reminds the reader that the son is a shared fantasy in Albee's original. And then, at the very end of the *Mad* version, Alfred E. Neuman strides in with books under his arm, cheerfully calling out something on the order of ''Hi, Mom! Hi, Dad! I'm home from school!''

Now, why is this funny? (Well, I happen to think it's pretty damn funny. Go with me on this point.) Obviously, this wouldn't mean much to a reader who wasn't familiar with *Who's Afraid of Virginia Woolf?* The whole point of the joke is in triggering the expectation that, as in the original, the son will turn out to be imaginary and then violently contradicting this expectation by introducing a real son, and one who is the image of idiocy at that.

When the integrity of an atom is violated—that is to say, when it is split—a tremendous amount of energy is released. (This, of course, is the principle behind nuclear energy and the atom bomb.) Similarly, theatrical energy is released when the integrity of a dramatic work is violated. This is the function of parody: to get laughs by subverting a known work or the conventions of a genre. This the *Mad* parody does with a vengeance.

But this business of generating theatrical energy doesn't apply only to parody. *Anytime* you set up an expectation onstage and then violate it, you're liable to get a burst of theatrical energy.

For example, after years of exposure to the likes of *Perry Mason*, *Witness for the Prosecution*, *L.A. Law*, *Anatomy of a Murder*, and *The Jagged Edge*, most audiences can reasonably be assumed to be familiar with the conventions of a criminal trial. Members of the Monty Python company and Peter Cook were able to make use of this assumed familiarity in a trial scene in *Pleasure at Her Majesty's* (a filmed record of an Amnesty International benefit featuring many of the leading lights of British comedy).

A defendant, played by Cook, is brought up on charges of murder. Actually, on charges of multiple murder. The court clerk reads off the list of people the defendant is accused of having killed. The list goes on for pages, and the victims are identified as an incredible variety of nationalities working at an incredible number of jobs. The defendant is asked how he pleads. He says guilty. Everybody in the courtroom groans from disappointment. Not wanting to ruin their good time, Cook changes his plea to not guilty. "Jolly good!" says the judge. Someone observes that the defendant's counsel is not present. The judge says that doesn't matter, they can start without him. A minute or so later, the counsel, played by John Cleese, comes rushing in, full of apologies. With a burst of energy to make up for lost time, Cleese launches into virtuoso courtroom histrionics, pointing his finger and accusing Cook of the murders. "I submit you murdered these people!" says Cleese. Cook says he did. "Did you murder these people?" asks Cleese. Cook says that he did. Cleese perseveres. "Answer yes or no! D*id* you mur-der these people? Yes or no?" Cook says yes. "Yes or no?" Cleese bellows. Cook says yes. And finally, Cleese seems to have heard. "Aha! We've wheedled it out of you at last, have we!" And he laughs a maniacal laugh of triumph, whereupon the judge asks Cleese if he is entirely aware of the fact that he is the attorney for the defense. This brings Cleese up short. "Terribly sorry," he mumbles, and he swings into a defense. Later in the scene, Cook says something that the judge doesn't like, so the judge pulls out a pistol and shoots him in the arm. Cleese gets up in a rather matter-of-fact way and says, "Your Honor, I really must object to your shooting my client."

There's a lot more of this sort of thing. God knows I haven't done the scene justice, but I think it is a classic of sketch com-edy.

The reason it is funny has to do with our familiarity with the way a serious trial is conducted and the juxtaposition of this nonsense against that model in our mind. The sketch goes out of its way to violate almost every preconception we hold of the way a trial is conducted.

You don't have to violate a somber ritual to get a laugh. Vary-ing from the norm of even a small bit of routine can do the trick. In Billy Wilder's *The Apartment*, Jack Lemmon is seen preparing a spaghetti dinner for a guest. Nothing unusual about this, except that, in an attempt to entertain the guest, instead of straining the spaghetti with a strainer he uses a tennis racket. A small variation from the norm, a nice laugh.

This technique of setting up expectations and violating them can be employed for dramatic effect as well.

The trial scene I mentioned above is funny because of its violations of courtroom procedure. In the film *And Justice For All . . .* , the high point of the climactic scene is the moment when the attorney for the defense, played by Al Pacino, stands up in court and accuses his own client of being guilty of the crime for which he is charged. This is analogous to Cleese's defense attorney wringing a confession out of Cook's defen-dant, but in this instance, the result is very dramatic.

An example in the same vein—the television movie *Gideon's Trumpet*. Based on a real case, the film contrasts two trials of the same man on the same charge, the second trial serving to show by contrast how badly the defendant's rights were abused in the first trial. Again, the dramatic effect is the result of the second trial being at variance with the pattern established in the first.

To go to a less formal ritual, in Harold Pinter's *The Birthday Party*, two mysterious gangster types participate in the party of the title, but it is not like any birthday party anyone would care to attend. Under the surface of the alleged celebration, a small war of terror is being waged by these men against the guest of honor. The lights go out. When the lights come back on, the birthday boy can no longer speak. Afterwards, the two gangsters spirit the man away to an unmentioned but clearly unpleasant fate. A violation of the conventions of birthday parties to chilling effect.

In a previous chapter, I referred to three scenes in *Hamlet* in which rituals or conventions are violated: the presentation of the play-within-the-play, Ophelia's funeral, and the fencing contest between Hamlet and Laertes. In each scene, Shakespeare tells us to expect an event the normal course of which we know, and each time, he then purposefully breaches the course:

We expect a play to proceed uninterrupted—Shakespeare flies against this expectation with Claudius's frantic cry for lights in the middle of the performance.

We expect decorous behavior at a funeral—Shakespeare supplies instead two men who fight bitterly at the grave.

We expect sporting contests to be fair—Shakespeare presents instead a spectacle in which one of the contestants finds himself facing the unsporting odds of a poisoned sword and an opponent who is willing to go outside the rules of the match to prick him with it.

One of my favorite examples of a ritual being violated occurs at the end of the first act of *Fiddler on the Roof*. The scene is set up to be a joyous Russian Jewish wedding. The wedding begins strictly according to tradition. After the ceremony, one of the characters goads the men and the women into dancing together, which is definitely not according to tradition. This is the source of a good deal of comedy, building to the point at which the rabbi finds that even he is dancing with a member of the opposite sex! The conventions of a Russian Jewish wedding have been violated for comic effect.

Hard upon the heels of this moment, however, the Constable arrives with some men carrying clubs. A "demonstration" has been ordered. The Constable supervises as his men overturn tables, smash dishes and gifts, and club one of the guests. Another violation, another explosion of dramatic energy—only this time the violation results not in comedy but in a moment of compelling drama. *Fiddler*'s book writer Joseph Stein has adroitly employed the violation of the same ritual to both humorous and serious effect.

Part of the purpose of drama is to question and challenge the assumptions of our lives. Turning familiar rituals and conventions upside down can be a very effective way of accomplishing this, for doing so causes the audience to look at the values implicit in them in a fresh way.

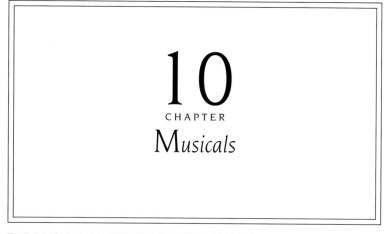

10

CHAPTER

Musicals

THE MUSICAL IS OFTEN DISMISSED BY MANY WHO FANCY THEM-
selves "serious" theater people as the theatrical equivalent of
a Twinkie—enjoyable but not very substantial—certainly the
last place to look for a dramatic exploration of serious ideas.

I think this is an unfair characterization. More often than not,
the memorable musicals have dealt with substantial social
themes. In fact, the very *form* of the traditional large-cast musical virtually dictates the exploration of social themes.

For years, it was a given that a Broadway musical had to have
a chorus. The musical function of a chorus is to sing together.
People ordinarily don't harmonize and share words unless they
share values. Usually, then, the chorus represents a community, whether it's the citizens of the state-to-be in Rodgers and
Hammerstein's *Oklahoma!*, the office workers of Frank Leosser
and Abe Burrows's *How to Succeed in Business Without Really Trying*,
or the Londoners of Stephen Sondheim and Hugh Wheeler's
Sweeney Todd.

The soloists, by definition, sing music different from that
sung by the chorus. It is logical, then, that the soloists' characters would tend to have values different from those of the chorus. It is logical, too, that this difference in values would lead to
conflict between the individuals and the community. There are
two possible resolutions to the conflict between the individual
and the community—either the parties reach an accommodation or one (usually the individual) is separated (usually in the
form of death or exile) from the other.

This, with variations, describes the basic thematic spectrum of most of the classic musicals: at one end, the shows in which images of accommodation or conciliation dominate, at the other, those emphasizing images of separation or destruction. Most of what are generally agreed to be the basic works in the canon have upbeat endings, and so they emphasize the comforting news that conflicts between the individual and society can be settled happily.

To move from abstraction to example:

Meredith Willson's *The Music Man*. The leading character, Harold Hill, confronts not one but two communities. One is the brotherhood of traveling salesmen, which disapproves of his methods because he gives them a bad name. (They articulate this in the celebrated opening number.) The other is the populace of River City, who articulate their grim, stiff-necked credo in the song "Iowa Stubborn." Representatives of both communities attempt to destroy Hill during the course of the show. In the town, Marian (the librarian) and the Mayor sense that Hill is not what he represents himself to be, and they work to get the goods on him and expose him. By the end of the first act, Marian has fallen in love with Hill and switched sides. Then the community of traveling salesmen actively enters the battle in the person of an anvil salesman who tells the people of River City the unappealing facts about Hill. At the show's end, Hill and the townspeople have reached an accommodation when he turns out to be not quite the fraud even he thought he was. When the curtain comes down, we know he is a reformed character and will settle down among them with Marian.

Marian, too, is in conflict with the community. She doesn't get along very well with the other women, as evidenced by the song "Pickalittle," in which they complain of her highfalutin' tastes ("Chaucer, Rabelais, Balzac!"). In another number, the "Piano Lesson," Marian and her mother have an argument in which Mrs. Paroo tells her daughter that she'll never get the respect of the town as long as she is unmarried (remember, the show is a product of the 1950s) and disdainful of other people's tastes. By the end of the show, Marian has found herself a man and has learned a little tolerance.

And the town has moved a little, too. It recognizes the contributions Harold Hill has made and forgives him his trespasses. It also has lost its grimness and has begun to have something of a cultural life. The same ladies who expressed their disapproval of Marian's literary tastes in act one are themselves shown to be entranced by Chaucer, Rabelais, and Balzac in act two.

If *The Music Man* is a prime example of a musical dealing with accommodation, the Leonard Bernstein/Stephen Sondheim/ Arthur Laurents/Jerome Robbins collaboration, *West Side Story* (which premiered the same year, 1957), represents the opposite end of the spectrum. The tribal, combative ethic of the Jets and Sharks is laid out in the opening ("When You're a Jet"), the dance at the gym, the war conference in Doc's store, and, of course, the rumble. When Tony and Maria challenge this ethic by falling in love, they find that they cannot overcome the hatred that shapes the world around them. The values of their environment prevail, leading to Tony's death and the death of his best friend and of Maria's brother. *West Side Story* was one of the first great musicals to deal with leading characters who are destroyed by their society. (*Sweeney Todd* is the other great example. Of course, grand opera, with all of its climactic murders, suicides, and fatal illnesses, commonly employs the images of separation and destruction—think of *Carmen*, *Otello*, *La Traviata*, and *Don Giovanni*.)

Between the two extremes that *The Music Man* and *West Side Story* represent are the shows in which elements of both accommodation and destruction appear:

In *Brigadoon*, Tommy, the outsider, is assimilated into the town; Harry, the disaffected resident, dies trying to escape it.

In *South Pacific*, Nellie and Emile are able to find happiness because of Nellie's ultimate rejection of her racist upbringing; Lieutenant Cable, unwilling to marry Liat and so challenge the values of the folks back home ("You've Got to Be Taught"), dies.

In *Show Boat*, Julie is separated from the community of the traveling company and Ravenal is ultimately integrated.

My examples come from the so-called golden age of musical theater, but the motifs of assimilation and separation continue in the big musicals of today. The Cameron Mackintosh and Andrew Lloyd Weber efforts, aspiring to high significance, tend to engage the latter; the title characters of *The Phantom of the Opera* and *Miss Saigon*, for instance, are both at odds with the choruses of those shows and both suffer as a result.

But the skyrocketing costs of musical production have led dramatists to write pieces requiring smaller casts, fewer or less elaborate sets, and fewer musical instruments. This in turn has had an effect on the themes of these projects. You are less likely to write a show about an individual in conflict with a community if you can't afford to put enough people onstage to effectively represent that community.

Two small-scale works produced at Playwrights Horizons in recent seasons give some indication of an alternative thematic focus for musical theater.

William Finn and James Lapine's *Falsettoland* has a wisp of a story, but its real *raison d'être* is to explore the dynamics of the odd *de facto* family that springs up around Marvin. Conventional plot disappears almost entirely in Craig Lucas and Craig Carnelia's underestimated jewel, *Three Postcards*, which juxtaposes the public behavior and the private thoughts of a trio of women at dinner together.

What these two shows have in common is the exploration of the interplay of a small community. Each is an ensemble show with a quasi-sociological focus, exploring the dynamics of a group or enclave.

I see the Stephen Sondheim/George Furth/Harold Prince collaboration, *Company*, as a key transitional work. I think the source of the problem some people have with this groundbreaking show is that it is caught between two thematic focuses. On the one hand, strictly speaking, it subscribes to the pattern of the leading figure being assimilated into the world represented by the chorus: By the show's end, an emotionally reborn Bobby is prepared to join the ranks of the ensemble as one who is finally willing and able to make a commitment to another person. On the other hand, though Bobby is the ostensible lead of *Company*, his passivity as a dramatic figure makes virtually every other character in the show more vivid. We don't see Bobby so much as we see the other characters *through* him. He is a dramatic lens through which the married couples he knows are explored. This exploration anticipates A *Chorus Line*, another show short on narrative and long on the investigation of a group; here Bobby's function is filled by Zack, the director for whom the dancers audition. Both *Company* and A *Chorus Line* climax with decisions by these lens characters. As I said above, Bobby decides to make himself open to commitment; Zack decides which of the dancers will get jobs in his show.

What *Falsettoland* and *Three Postcards* do is do without a lens character. Of course, this means doing without a lens character's decision as a means of resolving the central dramatic question. It's worth noting that not building to a strong climactic decision, neither attempts to sustain more than one act (though *Falsettoland* and its one-act predecessor, *March of the Falsettos*, were subsequently paired on Broadway as a two-act show called *Falsettos*).

I'm not saying that this is *wrong*. There is no rule that a musical has to be two-and-a-half hours long with eight sets, an overture, a dream ballet, and dancing villagers. I submit these comments by way of observing that the musical is evolving and to suggest in what direction this evolution is going.

In previous chapters, I've supported some of my theories with examples from musicals, so it should come as no surprise when I say that many of the same principles that govern ''straight'' plays govern musicals.

For instance, just as there are character-structured and event-structured plays and films, there are character-structured musicals and event-structured musicals. *Pippin* is a character-structured musical, taking its form from the title character's quest. A *Chorus Line* is an event-structured musical, taking its form from an audition. *Gypsy* is a character-structured musical, taking its form from Rose's pursuit of her dreams. 1776 is an event-structured musical, taking its form from the actions leading to the signing of the Declaration of Independence.

Lehman Engel drew parallels between the conventions of the contemporary musical and those of Shakespeare's plays. In contemporary "straight" plays, it is hard to make an audience buy a soliloquy. Of course, this is a convention we accept in Shakespeare. It is also a convention we accept in musicals. Except in a musical the soliloquies aren't spoken but are in the form of songs. When sung, we don't challenge the articulation of internal thoughts.

Take "Rose's Turn" in *Gypsy*. I can't imagine Rose standing onstage alone and *saying* these things. But the song gives her license to tear into the frustrations that have been building throughout her life, and it makes for a stunning piece of theater.

Again, to put Billy Bigelow alone onstage to talk to himself about his expectations for his unborn child would run the risk of being comic. But, in the form of a song, not-so-incidentally titled "Soliloquy," this is one of the high points in *Carousel*.

The opening number of a show carries particular weight. It acts as a kind of contract with the audience. It sets the style for the evening and tells us what to look for. You can kill a show with the wrong opening number.

I've already related the story about how Jerome Robbins helped Stephen Sondheim and company arrive at the appropriate opening for *A Funny Thing Happened on the Way to the Forum*. Look at the other great musicals, and you'll see that their openings take pains to set your expectations for what is to follow, usually through a musical number. "Another Opening, Another Show" promises a show about show people, and *Kiss Me, Kate* delivers. "Tradition" promises a show about trying to hold onto prized values in the face of adversity, and *Fiddler on the Roof* delivers. "Wilkommen" begins with a cynical greeting from a master of ceremonies who looks like death and what follows in *Cabaret* is a portrait of the moral decay of Berlin in the 1930s.

Writing lyrics for the theater is a substantially different discipline from writing lyrics for pop songs. Pop songs frequently are direct and explicit statements about the singer's condition. "You Made Me So Very Happy," "I Can't Get No Satisfaction," "She Loves You." This is fine for three or four minutes at a shot. But, as I've written, dramatic material by nature is implicit, urging the members of the audience to glean the truth for themselves rather than having it shoved down their throats. This is something that pop lyricists tend not to understand. The result is that when they try writing for the stage, some very accomplished pop lyricists have written some less-than-effective theater lyrics.

For example, in my opinion Hal David's lyrics for *Promises, Promises* are very flat. In songs like "Knowing When to Leave" and "Wanting Things," the characters stand around and exhaustively and candidly evaluate themselves. But this information is, for the most part, old news, making the songs dramatically useless. The key exception in this score is "I'll Never Fall in Love Again," in which even as the two leads protest their determination never again to get involved, we in the audience can see that a relationship is beginning between them. I don't think it's any accident that this has proven to be the most popular song in the score. I don't mean to put down Hal David; he has written some wonderful single songs with Burt Bacharach. But because he didn't understand the difference in the disciplines, his work on *Promises, Promises* does not approach his best.

I believe there are two essential talents needed to write lyrics. One is the ability to find the best point of attack for a song in a given dramatic moment. The other is to execute it well. To my mind, the first talent is the more important. No matter how sparkling the execution, if a song is weakly conceived, it won't add much to the show. On the other hand, the uninspired but workmanlike execution of a well-aimed song will still serve a musical's needs.

The glory of Oscar Hammerstein II was his extraordinary ability to discern what a song for a given moment should be about. He didn't have the panache of Richard Rodgers's previous collaborator, Lorenz Hart, or, indeed, other, technically flashier lyricists such as Stephen Sondheim and E. Y. Harburg. But if his rhymes rarely dazzled and delighted, and the forms he chose tended toward the conservative (and elicited the more conservative side of Rodgers), almost always the sense of his lyrics hit the bull's eye.

Whether or not he ever analyzed his craft as being a matter of premises and conclusions, it is a concept his work often brilliantly embodies. A lesser lyricist writing the scene in *Carousel* in which Billy Bigelow and Julie Jordan find themselves attracted to each other might well have tried a dead-on approach in which they sang something like, "Suddenly, here with you, I'm beginning to fall." Instead, Hammerstein wrote the extraordinary "If I Loved You." That "if" is crucial because it carries Billy and Julie's seeming denial of what we know is already happening in their hearts. As they explicitly deny their feelings, we in the audience smile because we know better. Hammerstein wrote similarly conceived and equally successful songs in "Only Make Believe" for *Show Boat* and "People Will Say We're in Love" for *Oklahoma!* Richard Adler and Jerry Ross echoed the technique in *Pajama Game* when they wrote "I'm Not at All in Love." Similarly, Sondheim had an overwrought Hysterium sing "I'm Calm" in *Forum*; Lionel Bart had Mrs. Corney pretend to protest Mr. Bumble's advances with "I Shall Scream" in *Oliver!*, and as I observed above, Hal David had Chuck and Fran swearing to each other "I'll Never Fall in Love Again."

One of the reasons Lerner and Loewe's score for *My Fair Lady* works so well is because almost all of the songs hew to the premises-and-conclusions model. In lyric after lyric, Lerner has the characters sing words that goad the audience to respond with conclusions significantly different from the lyrics' explicit content. Higgins sings, "I'm an ordinary man." The audience thinks, "Ordinary—hell! You're eccentric and very nearly insufferable." In "Just You Wait," Eliza sings of her desire to put Higgins up against a wall and order his execution. The audience thinks, "You don't realize it, but you're interested in him." After the ball, Pickering and Higgins congratulate each other, singing, "You Did It!" The audience is ready to shout out, "No, you idiots, *she* did it!" Eliza sings, "I can do very well without you." The audience knows better. Higgins sings, "I've Grown Accustomed to Her Face." We know that his feelings are a good deal stronger.

Thus, in song after song, the characters deny their feelings, incorrectly characterize them, or evaluate situations in ways that prompt members of the audience to respond with their own evaluations. If the audience responds, it necessarily is engaged in the material. (Only in "On the Street Where You Live" does a character explicitly articulate his feelings. It's pretty, but dramatically it is easily the least interesting part of the score.)

What I wrote about the power derived from violating rituals and routines also applies to musical theater. Some of the most effective moments in musical theater have come when a song or convention that has been established early in a show is reinvoked later but with a crucial change.

In *Fiddler on the Roof*, Joseph Stein, Sheldon Harnick, and Jerry Bock establish a convention in which, whenever he's faced with a daughter's unorthodox engagement, time freezes and Tevye carries on an internal debate. One the one hand, he says, there are certain rules and traditions. On the other hand, his daughter is in love. In each of the first two cases, he decides to bend and comes down on his daughter's side. When his third daughter, Chava, marries a non-Jew, time stops once more. The audience, conditioned by the previous two debates, thinks, "Here we go again" as Tevye goes through his "on the one hand/on the other hand" routine. Except this time he breaks the routine. "There *is* no other hand," he decides, and in a horrifying moment he banishes Chava from her family and community. The horror of the moment is reinforced by the violation of the convention established in the two earlier passages.

Again, in *Sweeney Todd*, Sondheim has Toby sing to Mrs. Lovett, "Nothing's Gonna Harm You" (the irony being that Toby perceives Mrs. Lovett as somebody who needs to be protected when, in truth, it is the rest of the world who could use some protection from Mrs. Lovett). Later, as Sweeney and Mrs. Lovett search for Toby, it is Mrs. Lovett's turn to sing "Nothing's Gonna

Harm You"—a chilling moment because we know that she and Sweeney are determined to kill him. Her cynical reprise of this song is an index of her betrayal of Toby.

Each character must be as clearly defined by his or her music as by the words he or she sings. For instance, in Sondheim's A Little Night Music, the soldier is characterized by a military polonaise. The old lady's song, "Liaisons," is written with a heavy impressionist influence. The lawyer's opening song, "Now," is crisp, evenly measured, and well reasoned—just what you'd expect from a good lawyer. By contrast, Henrik, his confused son, is characterized by an uneven, rambling melodic line—now hurtling impulsively, now halting. The melodic line for the lusty maid's song, "The Miller's Son," soars uninhibitedly. We would know a great deal about these characters if we heard *only* the music.

The writing of a musical is a balancing act. One constantly has to juggle and keep in proper proportion the elements of spoken material, song, and dance. In addition, one constantly has to be on guard against monotony. For instance, three romantic ballads in a row, even if they are beautiful songs, will not play effectively. If you listen to the cast albums of the great musicals, you will hear that from song to song there are major shifts in tempo, form, style, and/or the number of singing parts. Rarely will a solo song for one character be followed by a solo song for the same character. One of the reasons so many of the so-called rock musicals didn't work very well (*Via Galactica, Billy, Catch My Soul*, and numerous others too ephemeral to mention) was that the same beat in song after song made it impossible to differentiate the songs; the scores became large, ill-defined muddles of sound. Also, it became difficult to distinguish between characters because they were all characterized by the same musical language.

I can't pretend that in such a brief space it is possible to explore in detail all of the aspects of writing a musical. But if you take a look at the musicals that have continued lives, I believe you will find that though they tell their stories largely through song and dance, they do so in ways consistent with the principles that support successful plays.

11

CHAPTER

Screenwriting

MORE DRAMATIC WRITERS MAKE THEIR LIVINGS OUT OF WRITING screenplays or teleplays than out of works for the theater. That fact and the appeal of writing something that once produced will continue to exist in a finished form leads many playwrights to hope to write for the camera.

It's a logical move. After all, both playwrights and screenwriters attempt to tell stories primarily through the medium of actors' behavior. Virtually all of the techniques I've discussed are applicable to both the stage and screen. (You'll recall I've illustrated my theories with examples from theater and film, as well as television.)

But, though related, there are still some clear distinctions between the disciplines. I believe these distinctions account for why some very successful plays have been adapted into unsuccessful films, and why some very talented playwrights have not flourished in their attempts to write for Hollywood. Much of the difficulty has to do with the difference in scale. Films generally tell bigger stories than plays do.

By "bigger" I mean that movie stories are usually constructed out of more plot points. David Mamet has said that he needs dozens of plot points to build a screenplay, three or four of which might well be a sufficient basis for him to write a satisfying play. (Certainly there are a lot more incidents in his screenplay for *The Untouchables* than in his play *American Buffalo*, both notably effective scripts for their respective media.)

Why do movies tell bigger, more involved stories? Largely because they *can*. Editing grants movies a temporal and spatial mobility denied the naturalistic stage.

In film, in one twenty-fourth of a second, the filmmakers can shift from a shot featuring the leading lady stepping out of her bath to a shot of her made up, bewigged, and wearing a hoop skirt in preparation for a costume ball. Onstage, the script would have to incorporate a scene to engage the audience's attention for a minute or two while the actress dashes back-stage to be painted, bewigged, and Velcroed for the ball by a makeup artist, a hair stylist, and a dresser.

The shift from one realistic set to another is similarly no problem in a film. One second the filmmakers have you in a gondola on a canal in the Venice of Italy, the next they've got you listening to an animal-rights activist on the boardwalk of the Venice of Los Angeles. Onstage, even with the most sophis-ticated scene-shifting equipment, time must be taken for this sort of transformation. (Shifting nonrealistic sets onstage can be much quicker, courtesy of projections, the switching of key props, and lighting.)

The movies' comparative advantage in mobility encourages the use of a great many more scenes than are used in plays, often as many as a hundred or more. Because there are so many scenes, generally they are shorter; some are as short as a few seconds. In fact, these days film producers get antsy when they see more than two or three scenes as long as five pages in a feature script.

(Once upon a time, movies were allowed the luxury of longer scenes. For example, Jo Swerling and Niven Busch's screenplay for the 1940 cowboy movie *The Westerner* featured the requisite gun battles and fistfights, but it also had glorious extended pas-sages of black comedy between Gary Cooper and Walter Bren-nan. Today's producers insist that the members of today's audiences have been so conditioned by the pace of thirty-second TV commercials and flashily cut music videos that they wouldn't have the patience to sit still for such sequences any more. That's the rationale, anyway.)

Each scene of a screenplay, no matter how small, should have a dramatic purpose and should move the story forward another beat. Films therefore need a lot of incidents to justify their running times. The ones most successfully derived from the stage are based on plays that had a lot of plot points to begin with. Most of these plays either featured large casts or were episodic in structure.

As I've written before, the more characters there are in a play, the more potential for issues to be resolved between them, and, consequently, more negotiations and more plot. Jerome Lawrence and Robert E. Lee's *Inherit the Wind*, Sidney Kingsley's *Dead End*, Lillian Hellman's *The Little Foxes*, Lorraine Hansberry's *A Raisin in the Sun*, and Tennessee Williams's *A Streetcar Named Desire* all introduced more than four characters and had plenty of story to tell in their original form. All of these were transferred creditably. Though the film versions employed more sets than the original plays, there was little tinkering with the essential structures and major characters of the original scripts.

Other plays that have been the bases of relatively successful movies without having had much violence done to them generally have been those made up of a lot of small scenes and/or featuring several skips in time. Alfred Uhry's *Driving Miss Daisy* began as a small-scaled, three-character chronicle made up of many vignettes covering dozens of years; though Uhry added a few characters in writing the adaptation, he had the advantage of beginning with a play that already had a structure that lent itself to film. The Broadway version of Aaron Sorkin's *A Few Good Men* featured so many brief scenes that it seemed to be virtually in screenplay form from the start.

As I've stated elsewhere, the current market for plays encourages the creation of scripts requiring small casts and few sets. The smaller the size of the cast, the fewer potential issues there are to be resolved between the characters and the fewer possibilities of those plot points that a feature-length film requires.

The result is that most small-cast plays have troubled transfers to the screen. If they are transferred substantially intact,

they are likely to come across as claustrophobic and con-
stricted. Take the case of Marsha Norman's 'night, Mother, a
two-character, one-set play that packed sufficient power
onstage to win a Pulitzer Prize in the theater but, in its screen
incarnation, disappeared quickly.

The general tack, then, is to attempt to "open up" intimate
pieces by adding characters and incidents. The original version
of Terrence McNally's Frankie and Johnny in the Claire de Lune took
place entirely in one night in Frankie's apartment. The film
introduced as well the diner in which they worked, plus a company of colorful coworkers, and a great deal of material predat-
ing Johnny's visit to Frankie's apartment. I'm not saying this is
wrong. If the adapters are able to maintain the tone and intention of the original, more power to them. But frequently, this
opening up results in a dilution of the material.

Playwrights hoping to sell the film rights of their work are
faced with a conundrum. The movies favor large-cast, multi-set
pieces—precisely the scale of work the stage mostly cannot
afford to undertake. And the intimate pieces stage producers
embrace with enthusiasm don't tend to adapt well to film without being augmented in ways that threaten to obscure what
made the plays attractive to begin with. It's hard to write something that appeals to both markets.

Playwrights who would like to write directly for the screen
face a related problem. Because the theater encourages them
to build small worlds occupied by a handful of characters moving through a small number of plot points, they tend to find it
difficult to adjust to the frame of mind necessary to construct
bigger stories for film. Dramatists have been conditioned to
strive to compress action to a limited playing area and to limited time and to explore each plot point more exhaustively than
film has patience for.

When Hollywood hires accomplished playwrights, it is likely
to get people who know how to write individual scenes of depth
and flair. It is less likely to get people who know how to create
stories of a scope that sustains feature length. Playwrights have
to modify their craft if they hope to make the transition to
screenwriting. Though the techniques I've explored—

negotiations over objects, character structure versus event structure, roles in conflict, and so on—are relevant to screenwriting, they must be employed with an eye to the differing needs of the two forms of writing.

12
CHAPTER
The Right Space

IN CHAPTER 3, I DISCUSSED THE CONCEPT OF NEGOTIATING OVER space. I said that one of the ways the relationship between characters may be dramatized is by how the dramatist positions them in relation to each other and their surroundings.

There's another spatial relationship with which dramatists must be concerned: the relationship between the play and the audience. You can have a fine, well-crafted script, a first-rate cast, and a gifted and sensitive director and still go down in flames if your play is presented in the wrong venue. It behooves professional writers to give as serious attention to securing the proper stages for their work as they do to any other aspect of production.

To put it simply: A play is not equally good in all spaces. In fact, a play is not the *same play* in all spaces. This is the reason why a number of plays that have flourished off-Broadway have wilted when transferred to Broadway.

An example: Albert Innaurato's *Passione* worked wonderfully at Playwrights Horizons. The play takes place in the crowded Philadelphia apartment of an Italian-American family. The Playwrights Horizons stage being on the smallish side, the cramped nature of the space contributed to the sense of people being constantly on top of one another, which was so necessary to the farcical elements of the play. All in all, the Playwrights Horizons production was a hoot.

When it moved to Broadway, *Passione* flopped. Why? The script wasn't significantly different, and the cast was substantially the same. But because the stage was wider than at Playwrights Horizons and the house of the theater much larger, the sensation of claustrophobia, which had been so useful off-Broadway, was lost. The apartment was no longer the pressure cooker that made the characters' outlandish behavior not just possible but inevitable. Without that pressure, the behavior seemed forced, unjustified. On Broadway, *Passione* was received with indifferent reviews, most of the critics attributing their disappointment to the script. A script that had worked very well in a small theater worked less well in a large one. Too bad, because it's one of Innaurato's more engaging works.

I think, too, of David Mamet's *The Water Engine*. The play depicts the broadcast of a radio drama, and, when it opened at the Public Theater, the production team went to some effort to encourage the audience's sense of participation in the event. To create an informal and playful atmosphere, the house was turned into a cabaret; we sat around tables and were served quiche and coffee. No proscenium separated us from the action onstage. Instead of being a group of 1978 theatergoers, we were treated as a studio audience circa 1934. Before the play proper (which was a short work—about an hour, as I remember), singers sang to us and announcers plugged antique products at us. By the time the "broadcast" of the play started, we had been thoroughly primed to sustain with the company the illusion that we were temporarily escaping the Depression in this radio studio. Between the milieu created and the quality of the play itself (I think it is a fascinating and provocative piece; I was less taken with Mamet's padded made-for-TV movie adaptation), the evening was a delight.

The reviews of this production were nearly universally wonderful. Joseph Papp was understandably encouraged to move it uptown. As with *Passione*, the Broadway production employed the same cast and the same script, and again—a different event.

Instead of being seated informally around tables, the audience was seated in the formal rows of the Plymouth Theater. Because the Plymouth is a traditionally designed Broadway house, the play was framed by a proscenium, which undermined the illusion of the audience being in the same room and the same era as the actors. The sense of collaboration between the house and the performers, which had helped buoy the production downtown, was gone. What had been delightful off-Broadway seemed remote and austere uptown. The Broadway reviews—including some by the same critics who had praised the version at the Public—were unenthusiastic, and the show went under.

Sometimes it has worked the other way. Sometimes plays that have initially been presented in inappropriate spaces and died early deaths have found new lives when revived in spaces better suited to their values.

The original 1946 Broadway production of Eugene O'Neill's *The Iceman Cometh* at the Martin Beck—a proscenium house—received some appreciative reviews but ran only 136 performances. It wasn't until after O'Neill's death that the play received the production which established it as a classic: the revival under José Quintero's direction with Jason Robards as Hickey off-Broadway at the old Circle in the Square Theater on Sheridan Square (not to be confused with the current space of the same name on Bleecker Street).

Brooks Atkinson's May 9, 1956, review of the revival in the *New York Times* describes the role that designer David Hays's use of the space played in the success: "A few tables and chairs, a squalid bar, a flimsy door leading into the street, a handful of fly-blown chandeliers and a few ranks of benches for the audience—they are all part of the same setting and closely related on that account." As a result, Atkinson wrote, "The audience has the sensation of participating," adding that the production "seems, not like something written, but like something that is happening."

Contrast this with the revival in the late eighties. Again Quintero directed, again Robards starred. But this time they were working in a huge proscenium house—the Lunt–Fontanne. No chance of the audience feeling as if they were part of the same setting there! I have no doubt that the failure of that production is substantially attributable to the decision (undoubtedly made for economic reasons) to run in that cavernous space.

I believe the Lunt–Fontanne was also largely to blame for the flop Broadway production of 3 *Penny Opera* (as it was spelled for that staging), in which Sting starred. Contrary to most of the critics, I think there was little wrong with what went on onstage under the late John Dexter's direction. Given in a more intimate venue—the sort of house for which the work was originally written, the sort of house that it played in for years off-Broadway (the de Lys, now the Lucille Lortel)—I am convinced it would have met with a much kinder reception. (Of course, in a smaller theater with a smaller potential gross, the producers wouldn't have had any hope of earning enough to pay Sting's salary.)

But then I think the Lunt–Fontanne is one of the least attractive theaters in the city. The last time I recall it playing host to a long-running drama or musical show (as opposed to a concert presentation) was the original production of *The Rothschilds*. And I'm not alone in thinking that *The Rothschilds* played much better in revival off-Broadway in a three-quarter round arrangement.

So playwrights facing production should examine their work with an analytical eye when consulting with producers, directors, and designers. There are certain key questions that have to be asked.

Is the scale of the play correctly matched to the scale of the house? If it is a small-scaled play, you will probably want a venue sufficiently intimate that people sitting at the back of the house will be able to appreciate the nuances of the playing. I thought Edward Albee made a crippling error when he authorized the premiere of his beautiful chamber drama *All Over* to be produced in the huge Martin Beck. The script was swallowed up in that space. (When it was given in a more intimate house in London, *All Over* was a substantial critical success.)

What are the technical requirements of the play? Some plays require elaborate scenery, which makes doing them in the round or in extreme thrust very problematic. It would be very difficult, for instance, to do *Les Miserables* in the round—in the second act, the barricade would block the audience's view of half the action. Lillian Hellman's *The Little Foxes* requires a staircase on which Horace may expire—also difficult in the round. If you've written a play that requires putting onstage two stories of a home—such as Neil Simon's *Broadway Bound* or Arthur Miller's *Death of a Salesman*—you're probably going to need a space with a high ceiling.

What is the optimum relationship of the play to the audience? If you want the performers to have a fairly casual relationship with the house, you'll want a less formal arrangement. I never understood, for example, why former Second City producer Bernard Sahlins kept trying to put editions of his company's revue into proscenium houses in New York. The company was formed and flourished in Chicago in a cabaret setting where people eat and drink and feel comfortable about shouting out suggestions for improvs. Obviously such an informal atmosphere is difficult to create in, for example, the Royale Theater. Similarly, much of the power of John Malkovich's production of Lanford Wilson's *Balm in Gilead* came from the blurry line between the audience's territory and the players'.

A diamond must be placed in the proper setting for its facets to be seen to best advantage. The same for a play. If you care about the work you've created, you must make certain that the audience meets it under the right conditions. This, too, is part of the playwright's responsibility.

13

CHAPTER

The Literal and the Metaphoric

AS A RULE, I DON'T BELIEVE IN EDITORIALIZING IN THE TEXT OF MY plays. In *The Value of Names*, I made an exception.

Early in the action, Benny Silverman finds himself in an argument with his daughter, a young actress named Norma. Norma has landed a part in a new play. Benny has read the script and is upset to see that the part requires her to appear topless. Norma defends the scene.

NORMA. That moment you keep harping on is about vulnerability.
BENNY. In your mind it may be about vulnerability. Maybe in the
    playwright's mind. In the audience's mind it will be about tits. The
    women out there will be thinking, 'Gee, I couldn't do that. Well,
    maybe I could do that. But how many margaritas would it
    take?' Meanwhile, the guys in the audience will be thinking . . .
    Well, you *know* what they'll be thinking. And their wives will know
    what they're thinking. And the women'll look at their husbands
    like they're saying, 'Yeah, and what are you gawking at?' And the
    guys will go, 'Hey, I'm not gawking.' And the women'll go, 'Oh,
    yeah, right.' And the guys will go, 'Hey, but it's OK: This isn't tits,
    this is art. I'm having a catharsis here. Swear to God. And yes,
    honey, I really do like yours better.' You're up there acting your
    heart out, and in the meantime, they've forgotten your char-
    acter's *name*.

There are a lot of things Benny says in the play that I don't agree with. This isn't one.

I don't believe that nudity works on the stage. I don't believe that there is anybody so pure at heart who sees a nude actor onstage and thinks, "That character is naked." No, the thought is, "That *actor* is naked." And as soon as the audience is thinking the word "actor," the illusion for which the actor has worked so hard, of disappearing into a character, is destroyed.

Several years ago, Diana Rigg and Keith Michell came to Broadway in a play called *Abelard and Heloise*. The play called for them to appear in a nude scene. Now, aside from being an actress of extraordinary talents, Diana Rigg is rather staggeringly beautiful, and I had had a crush on her since watching her on TV in *The Avengers*. When she wandered onto that stage (that *dimly lit* stage, I might add) in the altogether, I wasn't thinking about Heloise. Nor, I guarantee you, was anybody else in that audience. Similarly, the "ooh's" that accompanied Vanessa Redgrave disrobing in Peter Hall's revival of Tennessee Williams's *Orpheus Descending* had more to do with admiring the shape that Redgrave, somewhat north of fifty years old, was revealing than the poetry of Williams.

Similarly, I had a problem with the nude scene in Peter Shaffer's *Equus*. In John Dexter's production, everything else in the play was decidedly metaphoric. The set was an empty space in the round defined by railing that served scenes set in a variety of locations, and the horses were suggested by actors with masks and stylized hooves. Only when the girl in the stable attempted to initiate the boy sexually did the production go literal; their clothes came off and the audience began to wonder if the actor was going to manage an erection on cue. And suddenly the horses were just some members of Equity wearing masks and iron shoes again.

The theater is metaphoric by nature. Rooms mostly have only three walls. Time rarely corresponds to what our clocks measure. Lights shift to emphasize different areas according to the dramatic needs of the moment rather than being in strict response to characters throwing light switches, and they splash across the stage in colors unknown in our homes (or do the lamps in your place use gels?). Musical instruments often accompany action without literal justification. All this is palpably unrealistic, yet, when it's all working the way the creators hope, the audience *believes*. Toss something too realistic into the middle of this, the metaphor evaporates.

I'm not talking only about nudity.

At the performance of David Rabe's *Streamers* I saw, the murders at the play's climax were so realistically staged by Mike Nichols that a woman in the audience became hysterical. As she left the theater, I'm sure I was not the only one concerned about her well-being. I'm also sure I was not the only one who thought, "Gee, that's only stage blood up there." All of us who entertained these thoughts were out of the play.

During the Playwrights Horizons' off-Broadway production of Albert Innaurato's *Passione*, one of the actors cooked up some Italian sausages. The smell wafted through the theater, and a couple hundred theatergoers began to drool. Nothing metaphoric about that sausage. Nothing metaphoric about our response. And for those moments while we were salivating, we lost the illusion of being in the cramped apartment of a South Philadelphia family. We knew we were on the other side of the proscenium from a group of actors who were about to make us watch them eat a meal. And while we watched the food cook, we thought, "Gee, they've run a gas line up there!"

Animals onstage, too, break the illusion. When you have a real dog up there, half the audience is secretly hoping it'll heist a leg on the scenery. If it does, there will be nothing metaphoric about the resulting puddle.

Whenever something *too real* appears on a stage, the spell is broken.

The movies are a different matter. Most movies are designed to counterfeit the literal. You have real cars on the screen, real explosions, ingeniously faked bullet wounds, and space ships. A dog that would arrest an audience's attention in a play would excite no great comment in a film. We barely notice when characters cook and eat in a movie. And nudity is not as big a deal. (Though, confess, watching *Body Heat* don't you momentarily think, "*That's* what William Hurt and Kathleen Turner look like naked!")

The differences between stage and film are most apparent when comparing a film version of a play to its original stage incarnation. In contrast to the seduction scene in *Equus* onstage, the same scene in the film was not jarring. Of course, in the film the horses were "played" by real horses. With the loss of the masked and hoofed actors, the piece lost its under-current of ceremony and religiosity and with it a whole level of meaning. Whereas onstage *Equus* was an exploration of the nexus of psychosis and myth, on film it was just an artsy case history.

Having inveighed against nudity onstage, I have to admit there is one circumstance under which I have no objection — when a play is hopelessly tedious, I don't mind if an attractive actress throws her clothes and inhibitions to the wind. But I'm not going to represent this as a reaction that has anything to do with the appreciation of art.

14
CHAPTER
Ethics

AS PLAYWRIGHTS, WE DESIGN BEHAVIOR FOR THE STAGE. Through our scripts, we prescribe sequences of actions for the actors to bring to life, actions that are presented for the audience's consideration.

The audience looks at *Streetcar*'s Stanley Kowalski and is appalled by his brutality. It looks at *Gypsy*'s Mama Rose and is awed by the fierceness of her determination. It looks at *Twelfth Night*'s Andrew Aguecheek and is amused by his cowardice and stupidity. It looks at *Born Yesterday*'s Billie Dawn and admires her spirit. This is part of the audience's job—to evaluate the characters of the *dramatis personae* by the things they do. All of us make these sorts of judgments about those whom we encounter in daily life; naturally we make similar judgments when we watch a play.

Just by virtue of talking about judgments and the evaluation of behavior, we are entering the realm of ethics. The study of ethics focuses on the quality of choices human beings make and discerns whether these choices are admirable or contemptible, constructive or destructive, honorable or corrupt, and so on. As the theater is concerned with the depiction of behavior, and as the stock-in-trade of dramatists involves creating this behavior for the audience to evaluate, by its very nature the theater is an ethical medium and dramatists are, perforce, moralists.

This is most apparent in plays such as *All My Sons* and *Tartuffe*, whose authors wear their judgmental natures on their sleeves. Arthur Miller and Molière virtually issue indictments against their flawed central characters. *All My Sons* censures

Keller for his pursuit of business at the cost of his responsibilities to humanity at large. ("They were *all* my sons," he finally realizes before he heads offstage to commit suicide.) The title character of *Tartuffe* is portrayed as the embodiment of hypocrisy, and his unmasking and downfall are applauded.

But a play doesn't have to attempt to scale the peaks of Serious Art to make an ethical statement. E*very* play, no matter how trifling, fluffy, or seemingly brainless, implicitly offers judgments about human behavior. Neil Simon's *Barefoot in the Park* is a delightful confection, but between the laughs and the bits of business, it has something to say about the necessity of compromise and resilience to make a workable marriage. Kaufman and Hart had little more on their minds than to draw an affectionate caricature of their friend Alexander Woollcott when they concocted Sheridan Whiteside for *The Man Who Came to Dinner*, but even as we enjoy Whiteside's barbs and wisecracks, we can't help but view him as a bully with the capacity to do genuine damage.

Though moral matters are palpably dramatists' stock-in-trade, very few playwrights seem to have any training in ethics. This strikes me as curious. We accept that it's a good idea for lawyers and doctors to take courses about the proper employment of their skills. Yet, here we are in a society in which so much of people's moral concepts are absorbed from dramatic works, and little thought is given to the ethical education of those who write these works. I haven't heard of any playwriting program or drama school where ethics is a required course of study.

Bringing up the subject of ethics around dramatists is liable to make them put up their guard. A few years ago, Christopher Durang, Donald Margulies, Wendy Wasserstein, and I had a conversation on this topic for the *Dramatists Guild Quarterly*. Freshly burned by the hue and cry over his *Sister Mary Ignatius Explains It All for You*, which some found offensive to Catholics, Chris noted that an appeal to morality is frequently the tactic repressive forces use in justifying censorship.

But when I talk about ethics in writing, I'm not talking about fashioning propaganda or producing works tailored to meet the standards of some "right-thinking" committee. I'm talking about being aware of the values implicit in your work—understanding that whether it is explicitly articulated or not, your play can't help but rest on a philosophical foundation, can't help but give dramatic form to a system of belief or a perspective on human nature.

In the case of *Sister Mary Ignatius*, yes, a lot of people were upset by it. A lot of people, too, were upset by Wallace Shawn's *Aunt Dan and Lemon*. But as outrageous as they are, I think both are demonstrably moral works. Both Aunt Dan and Sister Mary Ignatius use their positions of authority to poison the minds of young people trusted to their charge. To expose their brands of miseducation strikes me as an inescapably ethical act.

Writing ethically doesn't necessarily mean having a character articulate your personal values in a resounding, well-phrased speech à la Ibsen or Miller. Part of what is intriguing about *Aunt Dan and Lemon*, for instance, is that *nobody* gives the speech that stands for what Shawn himself would say. Instead, he presents these sad, awful people to goad us to react against them. The vaccine for a disease is sometimes created by introducing a weakened version of the illness so as to stimulate the buildup of antibodies in the system. To my mind, that is what Shawn does in *Aunt Dan*—he introduces his title characters precisely so that we *will* be appalled by them and so that we will be particularly alert to those we encounter outside the theater who articulate similar garbage. (As it happened, when it premiered, some in the audience didn't understand the difference between depicting characters and glorifying them. Shawn found himself in the ironic position of being accused by some well-intentioned but obtuse souls of championing the very values he'd written the play to attack.)

I hasten to add that when I use the word "ethical," I'm not using it as a synonym for "inoffensive." Sometimes to offend *is* an ethical act. Some people and institutions roundly *deserve* to be offended. Satire that doesn't offend its targets is hardly worthy of the name. Lenny Bruce, now viewed as one of the icons of American satire, wasn't hounded by the police because they liked what he said. Chaplin didn't create *The Great Dictator* in the spirit of a Friars' roast; he wasn't out to give Hitler a good-natured ribbing ("But, all kidding aside, Adolf—"). And I'm sure Jules Feiffer's work didn't sit well with Richard Nixon and Lyndon Johnson, both of whom he attacked regularly in his cartoons. I'll bet that if Nixon or Johnson had responded by inviting him to the White House, Feiffer would have felt he was doing something wrong.

Many writers claim that they write for themselves, but, as I've said before, writing dramatic material is a social act. We write in the hope that what we create will be performed by actors for an audience and will stimulate a reaction in that audience. We must accept that part of our responsibility is to give serious consideration to what reaction—besides applause—we stimulate. Technical virtuosity is not a good in and of itself. After all, German director Leni Riefenstahl dazzled audiences by pioneering cinematic techniques, but can one overlook the fact that in *Triumph of the Will* those dazzling techniques were in the service of extolling Hitler and his philosophy?

The dramatist's job is further complicated by the fact that increasingly audiences are depending on images and information from plays, films, and TV in their attempt to comprehend the world. An example:

We all have a pretty fair idea of what happens in a trial. We know the prosecutor and the defense lawyer make opening statements and the prosecution presents its case through a parade of witnesses and the defense attempts to raise doubts about the prosecution's version by cross-examining those witnesses and, after the prosecution rests, the defense summons other witnesses to offer testimony challenging the prosecution's version of the events, these witnesses in turn being subject to the prosecution's cross-examination. And we know about closing statements and the judge charging the jury and the jury being sequestered and the reading of the verdict and about objections and lawyer-client privilege and the right to not incriminate oneself and lots and lots of other legal concepts and procedural details.

We know all these things despite the fact that relatively few of us have gone to law school much less have had direct exposure to a murder trial. We have gleaned our legal education from L.A. *Law*, *Witness for the Prosection*, *The Defenders*, *Anatomy of a Murder*, *Law and Order*, *The Paper Chase*, and *My Cousin Vinny*, among the hundreds of other *de facto* seminars on the workings of the judicial system we've attended in the quest for entertainment.

Earlier in this book, I theorized that the theater partially arose out of journalistic impulses—the desire of members of a tribe to share with other members the accounts of events of the community's history as well as its values, frequently in mythic form. In fact, I believe that originally theater *was* a form of journalism.

These days, we claim to make distinctions. Supposedly journalism is the presentation of facts by confident-looking people sitting behind desks on news programs or is marshaled into columns of type crammed between ads in the newspaper. In contrast, theater and its offshoots involve the talents of actors attempting to bring to life a story that usually began in a writer's imagination.

Despite these supposed distinctions, much of what people *think* they know about society and history is gleaned from dramatic material. The more real entertainment *looks*, the more credibility the audience invests it with, sometimes to the point of confusing the fictional and the factual. Oh, on a conscious level people may insist that they're smart enough to draw the line between art and reality, but years of dramatized images of lawyers and doctors and cowboys and cops and soldiers have inevitably influenced the audience's view of the way their real-life counterparts function in actuality. (During his presidency, Ronald Reagan habitually supported his positions by referring to vivid anecdotes. On more than one occasion, these events proved to be derived not from life but from old movies!)

If it is true that the audience is drawing much of its understanding of the world from entertainment, then I feel those who write the scripts should do so with an awareness of the influence of what they create.

We can only make decisions on the basis of the data we have at hand. The wisdom of our decisions is necessarily dependent upon what information we believe to be relevant. If we are denied access to the truth—if it is withheld from us or distorted—we are by definition being denied the opportunity and the right to make informed choices.

This is why dictatorships always make it their first order of business to control not only journalistic outlets but the arts. Joseph Goebbels, the propaganda minister of the Third Reich, understood that whoever controls the dissemination of information—whether in reportorial or fictional form—wields enormous power in a society. He also understood that if you forcefully repeat a lie often enough, it comes to assume the weight of truth. Putting theory into practice, he took control of all of Germany's media outlets and kept them hammering out the same corrupt messages so as to unify the German people behind Hitler. Such opposition media as attempted to deliver corrective information and images were suppressed, and those behind them imprisoned or executed.

Now, we don't live in a society of such enforced homogeni-zation. Nor, despite the delusions of Pat Robertson and his ilk, is there a concerted effort on the part of America's artists to ram a program of liberal values down the population's throat.

But just because there isn't a conspiracy doesn't mean that there isn't a lot of misinformation bred by ignorance, laziness, or the desire to sell tickets.

In his film *Mississippi Burning*, director Alan Parker presents an exciting picture of heroic F.B.I. agents battling on behalf of oppressed blacks in the South of the 1960s. In fact, however, the F.B.I. had scant sympathy for the civil rights movement. What little the F.B.I. did to further the cause of black enfran-chisement was done with great reluctance and largely because the Kennedy administration lit a fire under the agency. These facts were pointed out by many outraged commentators when the film was first released.

Parker and his collaborators responded, ''Hey, chill! This isn't a documentary, it's an entertainment! What are you getting so het up about?'' The reason a lot of people got so het up was that having established the world of the segregated South in a way calculated to persuade an audience of its reality, the film goes on to misrepresent an important part of modern history. The film is so artfully made that young people who weren't alive in the 1960s might well be persuaded that what they are seeing is a reliable portrait of the dynamics of the civil rights movement.

History isn't just what happened when old calendars were on the wall; it is a large part of how we got where we are today. Our understanding of today must rest on our understanding of yesterday. To falsify the past is necessarily to lie about the present. This is why it is important to protest the idiots who claim the Holocaust never happened. This is why any attempt to deal with today's racial tensions must acknowledge the degree to which we are still living with the consequences of centuries of slavery.

It is also important not to misrepresent today's world. *Pretty Woman* is an entertaining fairy tale, but it is disturbing to see prostitution on Hollywood Boulevard depicted as a legitimate road to true love (with a millionaire, yet!). One would never guess from this movie (or from *Risky Business* or *Night Shift*) that the hooker's life is more likely to be characterized by abuse, exploitation, addiction, disease, and early death.

Given the credence members of the audience give the stuff we dramatists write, I believe we have a responsibility not to consciously mislead.

To some degree our level of responsibility depends on the contract we've made with the audience at the beginning of the script. (You'll recall I introduced the idea of the contract with the audience in Chapter 6.)

A piece that begins with battles in outer space between various species of intergalactic creatures is clearly signaling that it's operating in a universe in which earthbound belief in certain laws of physics should be checked at the door.

A piece that begins with a gritty, semidocumentary tone is signaling that what is being portrayed is meant to be taken as representing something that is within the realm of possibility in the world as we know it.

Obviously, we wouldn't hold these two different works to the same standard of credibility. But having invoked realism, the gritty, semidocumentary piece has an obligation not to violate its established level of credibility.

I think that those pieces that signal that they are meant to be taken as serious representations of the world should not have their characters—whether based on "real" people or not—behave in a manner inconsistent with what reasonable observers would agree is the truth.

A gross hypothetical case in point: an exciting, persuasively detailed movie set during World War II in which valiant Nazis risk their lives to protect Jews from vicious American troops. This would obviously be viewed as a travesty by audiences with even the most minimal understanding of twentieth-century history.

Ludicrous? Yes. But to those who participated in the civil rights movement in Mississippi in the 1960s, *Mississippi Burning* is nearly as ludicrous. To Native Americans, the portrayal of American Indians in hundreds of old Westerns is similarly upsetting.

This kind of distortion is not new. Shakespeare was a great dramatist, but woe be the history student who answers questions on his final exam with information derived from *Richard* III. Shakespeare presents Richard as a misshapen, murderous tyrant. In fact, historians agree that Richard was not physically deformed and that rather than being a hated despot, he was something of a reformer and was popular with most of his subjects. And how about Shakespeare's *King John*? It's a wonderful black comedy, but it doesn't even bother to mention him being compelled to sign a little thing called the Magna Carta. And *Henry* V presents its title figure as embodying all of the greatest virtues of English manhood, though scholars insist he was a vicious adventurer known for committing atrocities during his war in France.

To be honest, I can't pretend to be deeply outraged by Shakespeare's distortions (though there are those so upset by his depiction of Richard that they have joined the Richard III Society whose purpose is to rehabilitate their maligned hero's reputation). Little in today's public life is likely to be affected by the popular misapprehensions about the lives of medieval kings. I mention Shakespeare to point out the power of art to form persuasive images in the popular imagination.

And with power comes responsibility.

I think we have a particular responsibility when we claim to represent real people or real events, particularly those with contemporary reverberations. My friend Corinne Jacker, a playwright and screenwriter who won an Emmy for her script for *The Adams Chronicles*, believes that all plays, films, and movies should automatically be labeled fiction.

I understand her point, but I respectfully suggest that even though one can expect the audience to understand that artifice is necessary to transform historical events into manageable and coherent works for the stage and screen, this doesn't excuse the writer from the duty to not grossly misrepresent important matters.

I'm not insisting that one must hew absolutely to the record. My play *American Enterprise* deals with events in the life of George Pullman, the Chicago industrialist. In reality, Pullman had two sons and two daughters. I needed only one of each to tell my tale. As my focus was on Pullman's relationship with the people in the "model" company town he built and the crippling national strike that came out of his confrontation with them, I didn't feel I was doing serious injury to the audience's understanding of the events by pruning George's family. On the other hand, if I had represented Pullman as the soul of compromise and had portrayed him and the inhabitants of his town as having worked in harmony to resolve their disagreements without a strike, I would have been guilty of falsifying a major event in American history.

Very few people have read much about Pullman, so I can reasonably assume that the information the audience gets from my play will probably form the bulk of their knowledge about him. I wanted to tell an entertaining story, of course, but having selected a historical subject, I felt the responsibility to balance my desire to entertain with fidelity to the major facts.

Jerome Lawrence and Robert E. Lee presumably felt this responsibility sufficiently that in writing *Inherit the Wind*, they changed the names of Clarence Darrow and William Jennings Bryan to Henry Drummond and Matthew Harrison Brady. Though the play was evidently based on the Scopes Trial, by virtue of these changes, Lawrence and Lee were signaling to the audience that they had chosen to take liberties with the record and that the play should not be confused with history.

One of the catch phrases of the 1960s was "you are what you eat." This saying applies not only to what one consumes by way of food but also by way of ideas and images. I'm not calling for the abolition of fiction and fancy. I am suggesting, however, that given the sad fact that a large part of the audience— particularly of TV shows and movies—is unsophisticated and does little serious reading to offset what it absorbs from entertainment, it is incumbent upon us not to tell lies for the sake of dramatic expediency.

At this point I must add that I don't believe that a dramatist's ethical concerns stop when the show is over.

One of the reasons Martin Luther wrote his 95 Theses was to protest the Catholic church's practice of selling indulgences. In essence, the practice allowed people to purchase spiritual chits to offset accountability for sins—so many ducats (or whatever) for an indulgence for impure thoughts, so many for theft, so many for murder. (I wonder if they had sales. "Now through November 15th only, get two indulgences for adultery for the price of one! Plan ahead!") Of course, the more money you had, the more indulgences you could afford to purchase. If you were poor, you were under pressure to stay on God's good side the cheap way, by being good. But the indulgence system gave rich people the luxury of believing that as long as they kept forwarding sizable sums to the local bishopric, they could act miserably in this world and still be assured of entrance into the happier subdivision of the next.

I see evidence that some in the arts similarly believe that their talents and achievements place them under different moral obligations than so-called civilians. Though they may not overtly claim such, they feel that their intentions and accomplishments—their gifts to the world entitle them to the contemporary equivalent of indulgences for their less appetizing personal behavior.

To some degree, our society supports this double standard. How many times have you heard someone say something along the lines of, "Yes, he may be a bastard, but isn't his new play wonderful?" In so saying, the speaker is implicitly granting the dramatist under discussion a degree of immunity from censure by reason of having written something good. (Does that mean that the author of a lousy play is more answerable for lousy actions?)

Some artists justify their crummy behavior by invoking the romantic view of the artist as a kind of outlaw—standing separate from society, holding to different standards, marching to different drummers. There is an essential distinction to be made, however, between those who, out of conscience, choose lifestyles at odds with so-called societal norms and those who crown themselves with the artist's garlands and consequently feel little sense of responsibility to anything but their own work. In *The Writer's Chapbook*, an anthology edited by George Plimpton of excerpts from interviews from *The Paris Review* with literary figures, Faulkner is quoted as saying, "The writer's only responsibility is to his art. He will be completely ruthless if he is a good one. He has a dream. It anguishes him so much he must get rid of it. He has no peace until then. Everything goes by the board: honor, pride, decency, security, happiness, all to get the book written. If a writer has to rob his mother, he will not hesitate; the 'Ode on a Grecian Urn' is worth any number of old ladies." I only hope that Faulkner was in a satiric mood when he said this. To seriously subscribe to such a credo is to offer the artist a special license for hooliganism. Rather than believing that being an artist is an implicit license to ignore some petty ethical niceties, I hold to the idea that it carries with it an injunction to hew to a higher standard.

I raised the issue of the desired relationship between character and art in a scene in a play called *The Value of Names*. Emily Mann, who directed the premiere, had some trouble with this passage. "Come on, Jeff," she said, "honestly: If you found out that Charles Dickens fucked ten-year-old boys, would that make him any less of a writer?" My response: "It sure would change how I read *Oliver Twist*." (I put this exchange into the script and got a lot of satisfaction out of the size of the laugh it usually received.)

No, molesting boys wouldn't have made Dickens any less of a writer, but it would have made him a hypocrite. If his readership had learned that such a thing was true, it certainly would have affected his credibility and their receptiveness to his work. And make no mistake about it: Credibility was important to Dickens. Much of his purpose in writing was to dramatize some of the shocking conditions of his time so vividly as to galvanize his public to demand reforms. Aside from being a great novelist, he was a major influence in English social affairs. I doubt he would have had such influence if his life had been revealed to so thoroughly contradict the values expressed in his art. (To tell the truth, some aspects of his private life *were* unappealing; the way he treated his wife was pretty reprehensible.) It is precisely because of this that Woody Allen came to grief. He had made an impressive array of films as an avowed moralist. By taking up with his former lover's young adopted daughter, he undercut the claim to wisdom any moralist must have in order to have credibility.

Some of my friends insist that as artists are subject to the same temptations as all human beings, it is unreasonable of me to hold them to a higher standard than other people. But I maintain that certain jobs do carry with them heightened responsibilities. We are dismayed when cops turn out to be corrupt because it is their particular duty to enforce and uphold the law. We would be appalled to see doctors endorse a brand of cigarette because we would view it as a violation of their mission to promote people's health. In recent years, we have seen and accepted as fitting the ruin of evangelists who were discovered to indulge in the sexual no-no's against which they so bellicosely preached. Similarly, as writers arrogate unto themselves the authority to set up dramatic situations through which they implicitly make value judgments about human behavior, I don't think it is unreasonable to expect them to attempt to live by standards consistent with those they apply to their characters. It would be unseemly to compose a ringing jeremiad against corruption and then turn around and try to screw collaborators out of their fair share of the royalties. What would you look like if you wrote and co-produced a film supporting women's rights and then were discovered to consistently pay the women in your office less than the men?

Yes, there are and have been some great figures in theater and film whose offstage comportment could only be termed dismaying. I don't claim this comportment invalidates their accomplishments. Nor do I claim that they are inferior artists because their characters are wanting. But I refuse to accept the idea that their accomplishments should mitigate against their accountability for damaging others. Art is meant to celebrate life, not act as an alibi for a life lived in bad faith.

15

CHAPTER

Learning Experiences

IT OCCURS TO ME THAT NOW MIGHT BE AN APPROPRIATE POINT TO relate something of how my own professional experiences have led me to the theories and opinions I've been advancing.

Probably most influential on my thinking were the three years I spent researching and writing a book called *Something Wonderful Right Away* about Second City, the troupe I mentioned in the chapter on dialogue.

Founded in Chicago in 1959 and specializing in revues made up of comedy sketches, Second City is still going strong. Among those who spent significant time there (or at its less polished predecessor, the Compass) are Mike Nichols, Elaine May, Alan Arkin, Barbara Harris, Alan Alda, Paul Mazursky, Shelley Berman, Melinda Dillon, David Steinberg, Joan Rivers, Robert Klein, Richard Libertini, Valerie Harper, all of the gang from SCTV (which stands for Second City TV), and a substantial percentage of the *Saturday Night Live* actors and writers (both John and Jim Belushi, Dan Aykroyd, Gilda Radner, Bill Murray, Tim Kazurinsky, Mary Gross, Chris Farley) since the beginning of that show.

It was and is a theater that has no writers; that is, none in the conventional sense. As I wrote in the chapter on dialogue, Second City material originates not in somebody's typewriter or computer, but through improvisations based on audience suggestions. These initial improvs are then pulled into rehearsal and developed until they are sufficiently refined to offer to a paying audience. In its more than thirty years of continuous operation, Second City has generated thousands of scenes without the formal participation of a playwright, and many of those who began as actors there have gone on to also write and direct. I wrote the book partially to find out why this was so.

At the beginning of the project, I took several months of classes in improvisation with Sheldon Patinkin, a former Second City director. One day, as I was improvising a scene under his coaching, I realized that, yes, of course, what I was doing— in collaboration with my scene partner—was writing on my feet. Though no words were being propelled onto a page, what we were creating was nevertheless dramatic material. What's more, I realized that our improv had to meet the same criteria to engage and hold an audience's interest as does any scene by Williams, Chekhov, Shakespeare, Pinter, Molière, or Wasserstein. To be successful, it had to present characters behaving in compelling ways in pursuit of their goals.

I hasten to add that Second City–style improvisation is not just a matter of actors assuming bizarre characters and blurting out anything that bubbles out of their ids, any more than jazz is created by a bunch of musicians blowing their instruments any which way. In order for jazz musicians to jam, they must agree on a key, time signature, tempo, and chord progression among other things. A jazz combo is only possible given shared familiarity with these components of music.

Similarly, theatrical improvisation at Second City is based on a shared familiarity with the necessary conditions of dramatic action. The pioneering work in this area was by Viola Spolin, who wrote about her theories in the classic book *Improvisation for the Theater*. She formulated what she called theater games— noncompetitive structures through which actors together could address dramatic problems while playing. Spolin's son, Paul Sills, began rehearsals for Second City by training his company to play his mother's games. When it was time to improvise scenes, the actors did so with the security of a shared body of knowledge and experience—the dramatic equivalents of keys, tempi, time signatures, and chord progressions.

It was in Patinkin's classes that I realized that *the same principles* that support successful improvisations could be applied to writing scenes. With a slight shift of perspective, many of Viola

Spolin's games for actors could be adapted to challenges for dramatists. It was at this point I came to believe that playwriting is an extension of acting, and that much of what applies to the actor's craft applies to that of the dramatist.

I've extrapolated many of the theories I've advanced in previous chapters from lessons learned while playing improvisational games, and I often draw on the games when I teach. I find that while students may intellectually appreciate a theoretical point I make about dramatic technique, they really *get it* in the course of playing the appropriate game.

I may discuss using a well-chosen object onstage, for instance, in order to make vivid the relationship between the characters, but the validity of this idea truly hits home when a pair of students improvise a scene about, say, former roommates arguing over what belongs to whom on moving day. Inevitably, in the wrangling over the possessions—the tapes, the books, the pictures, personal gifts, and so on—the dynamics of the relationship emerge organically.

Working on *Something Wonderful Right Away* was helpful in another way. Most of the chapters are in the form of extensive question-and-answer interviews between many of the stars and stalwarts of the Second City troupe and me. The text is largely made up of edited transcripts of our taped conversations.

Well, as I've said earlier, when you transcribe conversations verbatim, you cannot help but learn lessons about how people use language when they speak. You absorb their verbal sense and rhythms through your ears; these are then analyzed and processed in your brain and transmitted down your arms and out your fingers—their speech is converted into your physical activity, so you experience it in a more profound way than just listening to it. This is one of the reasons reporters tend to write persuasive dialogue; they have spent much of their professional lives relaying the words of others and, in the process, have internalized a sense of the way people talk.

I have also found that years of writing about other people's work has helped me clarify aspects of my own. I have the good fortune to edit, in association with Otis L. Guernsey, Jr., the *Best Plays* annual, which gives me the opportunity to see most of what is produced on and off Broadway and to write at length on the key works of the season. It is, by definition, a critical job.

Now I believe that criticism should be more than adjective slinging. I don't think it is sufficient merely to attach the words "stunning" or "disastrous" to a piece of theater. Anybody can praise or sneer. The attempt to write real criticism must involve supporting opinions with analysis. If you are conscientious about articulating your reasons for liking this and not liking that, you will inevitably discover clues to your own aesthetic. After all, your opinions on specifics are necessarily extensions of your general principles. At any rate, this is what I've found in the years I have spent writing about others' plays. Discussing these specifics has helped bring these general principles into the light.

I have found this to be enormously valuable when working on my own scripts. To return to a subject raised in an earlier chapter, for instance, in play after play I covered as a critic, I noticed that the most passive and least interesting character onstage was the autobiographic figure, an alter ego of the author. This put me on my guard whenever writing characters who resembled me in any significant way. So my critic side passed along an insight that my dramatist side has found of practical use.

Improvising, transcribing, and writing criticism—I originally did none of these things for the express purpose of improving my craft as a writer, but I cannot overestimate what I think I have learned from them.

I have also been associated, in one way or another, with a variety of writing workshops—sometimes as a member, sometimes as a leader. Inevitably, I have emerged from the years of hurriedly scratched notes and coffee in cardboard cups with some thoughts on what circumstances make for a constructive group.

I had the luck to be admitted at age eighteen to the Broadcast Music, Inc. Musical Theater Workshop as a composer-lyricist when its founder, Lehman Engel, was at the height of his powers. Lehman believed that we could learn not only from him but from each other, so he would assign all of us to musicalize the same moment in a play. I remember one particular assignment—a song for an attempted seduction scene in George Axelrod's *The Seven-Year Itch*. The next week, sure enough, there were twenty or so songs drawn from the same few pages. Some of them were riotously funny. Some of them were absolute clinkers. Lehman led a detailed discussion of each, trying to isolate the reasons behind what made which what. Inevitably, we found that we learned from one another's mistakes as much as we did from the felicities. General principles on how to approach writing the comedy song emerged. It was also somewhat inspiring to see the variety of possible responses to exactly the same piece of material, to see how many very different songs could be drawn from the same text.

The next workshop with which I clocked significant time was a playwrights unit at the Actors Studio in the late seventies run by Israel Horovitz. He had chosen ten or twelve writers whose work interested him to meet regularly around a table in a back room. The rule was that everybody every week had to bring in five new pages of a play in progress. He hoped that all of us would finish at least the first draft of a new play by the end of the season. And so, indeed, we brought our weekly install-ments, distributed copies for cold readings, and then, under Israel's leadership, discussed the work.

I admired Israel's organization of the group. As he had planned, most of us completed new scripts by the end of the season. (Mine, *Responsible Parties*, premiered in Chicago, had a run at the Vineyard Theater in New York, and is published by Dramatists Play Service.) My reservations had to do with a human dynamic. Israel was also bringing in his own work, and if you had the temerity to criticize it, frequently he would retaliate by shredding yours in turn. I rarely knew whether his criticism of my and others' work was on the basis of craft (and nobody could deny Israel knew a hell of a lot about craft) or spleen. If you don't have faith in the integrity of the criticism, its useful-ness is diminished. Ultimately, in the middle of my second year there, I decided to resign from that group and try to organize a new one on different principles.

The immediate task was to find people to join me. This turned out not to be very hard. In my experience, virtually everybody in the theater knows at least one playwright working in undeserved obscurity. So I called established writers, directors, actors, and critics of my acquaintance and asked them who their favorite obscure talents were. Julius Novick remembered one of his students from SUNY at Purchase who had written some very promising short pieces. David Mamet suggested a young actress who had made her debut in the off-Broadway production of *Sexual Perversity in Chicago*.

I was determined to include actors and directors as well as writers in the group. Actors and directors tend to analyze from different perspectives than do writers. An actor will be more likely to concentrate on the logic of a character's through-line. A director will be particularly conscious of when a point can be made through a piece of business instead of with words. Playwrights lucky enough to get feedback like this may be spared a lot of grief in rehearsal.

When the group began, I wanted to call it the Negotiating Stage (referring to my theory that all scenes must be negotiations), but Anne Meara, who was a member for several years, instantly said, "That's the most pretentious fucking thing I've ever heard!" Someone else came up with the name the Writers' Bloc, and that stuck. Most of our early meetings were in members' living rooms, though at one point, the Circle in the Square Uptown generously offered us free space.

In coming up with the modus operandi of the group, I remembered interminable sessions of other workshops I'd visited that had been devoted entirely to one writer's play. Something that I think must be recognized is that there has to be a certain—well, to be crass—*entertainment* value to a workshop in order to keep members showing up. If every week you have to sit through another full-length play that, by definition, probably doesn't work, after a few weeks you begin to come up with urgent reasons for not coming—like defrosting your refrigerator.

So I suggested that there be a fifteen-minute limit to the amount of material each writer could bring each week. This ended up serving a few purposes. For one thing, a writer was much more likely to get specific notes on details if there was only fifteen minutes' worth to analyze. For another, it was possible to deal with six or seven pieces each session, which meant that quite a few people were actively involved every week. Also, returning to the entertainment factor, if you thought someone's fifteen-minute chunk was a soul-deadening bore, you could take comfort in the knowledge that it would soon be over and followed by something possibly more stimulating.

I had another reason for not wanting to deal with completed first drafts. It is my experience that once writers have reached that point in a project, they tend to succumb to what I call the Vietnam syndrome of playwriting. You may remember that one of the rationales offered to support our continued participation in the war in Vietnam was that we had lost so many troops there that to pull out would be an implicit admission that those lives had been lost in a futile cause. Similarly, when a playwright has achieved a first draft, even if the structure is demonstrably flawed, the fact that a draft has been completed in that structure makes the writer reluctant to admit that he or she has gone so far and so long down the wrong path. The emotional investment in that wrong path is so strong that the writer tends to neither welcome nor heed critical feedback.

So the Bloc made a policy to deal only with material genuinely in progress. If in the preceding week a writer had come up with seven pages of what might be a new play, he or she would bring them in to see what those pages communicated to a group of well-wishing but critical colleagues. Part of the fun of the workshop was checking in for weekly installments of a variety of different stories.

Even though I founded the group, I benefitted as much as any attending. Once I started work on what I was sure was a four-character play. I brought in first sketches featuring all four, and, for three weeks running, the response from my colleagues was the same—three of the characters were compelling, and the fourth was a stiff. They were right. The fourth was there merely to elicit stuff from the other three. So I reconceived the play as a three-hander. From then on, it was clear sailing. The resulting play was *The Value of Names*. It premiered at Actors Theater of

Louisville, ran six months in Chicago, had subsequent runs in Philadelphia, Buffalo, Hartford, Los Angeles, and New York (as well as a production in translation on Swiss radio!), and was optioned for television. It also brought me to the attention of TV and film producers, whose assignments have been my primary source of income since. I am reasonably certain that none of this would have happened if my friends had not given me the good advice to dump that fourth character.

In addition to our regular meetings, remembering how valuable my experience in Sheldon Patinkin's class had been, I began a sporadic workshop in Viola Spolin's theater games for Bloc members. Sure enough, the writers who came to the improv workshops swiftly made breakthroughs in their work. There was a new economy to their subsequent writing and a new awareness of the importance of behavior as opposed to talk.

At one of these sessions, someone suggested that we improvise to music. My instant reaction was that this was an artsy-fartsy idea, but I had learned from Second City director Del Close that the most constructive response is not, "No," but "Yes, and— ." In an effort to keep the work from lapsing into tedium and preciousness, I said, "Yes, and this is how we'll do it: We'll sit in a circle and, as the music plays, any one person in the circle may initiate a scene with any other person in the circle; no scene may go longer than six lines."

And so we played. And we quickly discovered the power of six lines—three pairs of exchanges between two characters. We were impressed by the amount of action that could be condensed into this form. Then an exciting thing happened: Instead of each six-line scene being contained unto itself, members of the group began building off of one another's little scenes. A whole community of characters developed—story lines were sustained, secrets were created, hidden, and dramatically revealed, ironies bloomed.

I had been trying to figure out a way to encourage the actors and directors in the Bloc to begin writing, and the six-line form suggested a method. At the next regular meeting, I proposed that everybody every week bring in a six-line scene. We would read these, one after another, at the beginning of each session with an important proviso: These scenes would not be subject to criticism so nobody could be bruised by the experience. I reasoned that almost anybody could come up with six lines. If your six played well, you'd get a little pop of encouragement. If they didn't, well, hell, they were only six lines anyway, what's the big deal?

And that was how a lot of people who hadn't seriously thought of being playwrights began writing. Every week we began with these little dramatic hors d'oeuvres. Soon many of the Bloc stopped restricting themselves to only six lines and indulged in the luxury of writing a page or two. And soon we began assigning ourselves topics to address. I remember the night we did our six lines on "first love." *Everyone* had something to write about that, and the six-lines section, which usually took no more than twenty minutes, ended up going for more than ninety. I have seen few revues that entertained and moved me as much as the material that evening.

Soon several of the people who had joined us with no intention of writing began writing in earnest. One of these was the actress recommended by Mamet, Jane Anderson. She subsequently took many of the pieces she originally wrote for the Bloc and assembled her own one-woman show. Norman Lear saw it and hired her to write for television. She then created and produced her own sitcom, *Raising Miranda*. Then she began writing plays. As I write, her work has been given major productions off-Broadway and at the Actors Theater of Louisville, the Pasadena Playhouse, the Williamstown Festival, and Long Wharf. Most recently she wrote a critically acclaimed HBO movie starring Holly Hunter and Beau Bridges, *The Positively True Adventures of the Alleged Texas Cheerleader-Murdering Mom*.

The guy Novick recommended, Donald Margulies, hasn't done badly either. His play, *The Loman Family Picnic*, was produced at the Manhattan Theater Club to mostly enthusiastic reviews. In the 1991–92 season, his *Sight Unseen*, also at Manhattan Theater Club, won sensational notices from virtually everybody, moved off-Broadway, was on the short list for the

Pulitzer, went on to several productions in the regionals, and was sold to the movies. His work as a playwright has in turn led to many film and TV assignments.

A third alumnus, Keith Gordon, has become a critically acclaimed writer and director of such independent films as A *Midnight Clear*. Other members have had productions in important nonprofit theaters in New York and around the country, in the process picking up major grants and awards. All in all, a very productive and happy group.

After a while, there was a bloodless coup; I was toppled from my throne as head of the Bloc and demoted to an equal. After licking my bruised ego, I was delighted to find myself one of a band of friends who continued to meet for almost ten years. The group finally gave up the ghost in New York, but Jane Anderson moved to Los Angeles and started a chapter of the Bloc that, at this writing, is still flourishing there.

Here's the kicker: It was run with no grants, no funding, no larger sheltering organization. It survived entirely on the most minuscule of dues—a couple bucks a month per person to cover the cost of coffee and pastries. If the Bloc proves anything, it is that you don't need much to begin and sustain a vibrant and productive workshop. All that is necessary is a handful of idealistic, committed individuals and a living room big enough to hold them and their enthusiasm.

16
CHAPTER

Practical Advice

TO BEGIN WITH, IT HELPS TO HAVE WRITTEN SOMETHING PRO-ducible. I'm not talking only about keeping the size of the cast down. I'm talking about removing reasons for potential produc-ers *not* to put on your play. Mindful of how difficult it is for an unestablished writer to get a production, when I was writing my first substantial straight play back in 1974, I organized the material precisely *to* make it easy and cheap to mount.

The idea for the script originated in something in the life of a friend: Her ailing father asked her to join him to review the books of his business so that after his death she would have sufficient understanding of his affairs to make intelligent deci-sions. I thought the activity of a father and daughter reviewing accounts together would make an appropriate occasion for a piece about the two of them reviewing more personal matters. The initial idea was to set the play in his store—maybe a book shop or a stationer's.

Then I thought about what that would mean for the designer. There are easier and cheaper things than to build a vaguely real-istic set counterfeiting a store. So as not to require a producer with limited resources to fill shelves with books or stationery supplies, I shifted the action to the old man's front porch. It is evening. Father and daughter have gone over his affairs that afternoon; now they'll talk about what they avoided talking about before.

Obviously there were other steps in the development of the play, but I ended up with a script that made very simple production demands: the suggestion of a porch, a small cast (three characters), a handful of easy props, and costuming that could be done out of the actors' closets. I was trying to write the best play I could, but, at the same time, I was trying to make it the least challenging play I could from a technical point of view.

The upshot? *Porch* is easily the most produced of my scripts. All told, since it was first given a staged reading as part of the "In the Process" series at the Arena Stage in 1977, according to statements from Samuel French, it has received more than eighty stagings. I'd like to think its popularity is due to the quality of the writing, but I know the fact that it is easy and cheap to mount doesn't hurt.

My second piece of advice is that you disabuse yourself of the notion that your job as dramatist ends with writing the play. Don't rely entirely on your agent to market your work. I'm not saying that a good agent isn't a great help, but looking back on the various productions I've been lucky enough to have, I am struck by the fact that the majority of them came about because of people I've happened to meet.

The theater is a social art. Theatrical professions are necessarily social professions. Yes, even playwriting, which requires you to sit alone for hours and weeks and months at a time, has its necessarily social aspect. After the solo struggle, you have to have sufficient social skills to deal with the directors, the actors, and other people involved in putting on your play. But also, you are more likely to get a play on if you take an active part in the theatrical community.

Some stories by way of illustration:

Years ago, in an effort to persuade the Dramatists Guild it could do more for its associate members, Gloria Gonzalez and I got the blessing of its then–executive director, David LeVine, to run an experimental Guild session in association with the Society of Stage Directors and Choreographers. The idea was to invite to the Guild offices a bunch of SSDC members looking for projects, where they would meet a bunch of Dramatists Guild members holding scripts and self-addressed, stamped envelopes. David was a bit skeptical. He didn't think thirty people would show up. In fact, to his surprise and ours, more than a hundred twenty did—a dozen or so were directors, the balance were eager playwrights.

Gloria and I improvised a format: We had the directors rise in turn, introduce themselves and discuss the work they'd done, where they'd done it, and what kind of scripts they were looking for now. After the directors' presentations, the playwrights were unleashed to approach the people who most interested them. I was particularly taken by a director named Sandra Hastie (the same woman with whom Stephen Johnson and I later improvised *Cover*).

Sandie and I became friendly. She read and liked my stuff and in turn introduced me to Nancy Rhodes, artistic director of an off-off-Broadway company called the Encompass. For reasons too involved to go into, eventually another director of Nancy's acquaintance, Nan Harris, ended up directing *Porch* as a second-stage project at the Encompass. Happily, Richard Eder, then the first-string critic of the *New York Times*, was in an adventurous mood during our run. He came to a Monday show, gave it a warmly appreciative write-up, and the play was launched. (Nan subsequently directed a successful production of it in Los Angeles and a revival in New York at the Lamb's Theater starring Jill Eikenberry.)

All this because of my impulse several months earlier to approach Sandie.

Another story:

I was visiting the O'Neill Center summer conference. One night, after dinner, I was introduced to Julie Beckett Crutcher, then the literary manager for the Actors Theater of Louisville. She had sent me some encouraging rejection notes, but we had never met. I invited her out for an ice cream. Over her cone, she mentioned her company was going to begin commissioning short plays. Would I be interested in receiving a commission? You bet. I wrote that piece and was asked to write another. It was to satisfy this second commission that I wrote *The Value of Names* and reaped the good fortune I've described before. All this—at least partially—because of the ice cream cone.

Earlier I wrote that the majority of my productions came about because of "people I happened to meet." That made it sound like luck. But, as the old saying goes, you make your own luck. I obviously didn't know which people I would meet at the Guild or the O'Neill, or, in fact, that I would meet *anyone*, but, it was a fair guess that people interested in new projects would gravitate toward those places.

Yes, a play occasionally gets plucked by a literary manager from a mountain of submissions. But if you were a literary manager, which would be more likely to catch your eye—a script by someone you've met and spent agreeable time with or a script by someone unfamiliar to you?

It's important not to overlook your actor friends. (If you don't have any actor friends, *make* some. If you don't love actors, why are you trying to write for them?) Actors are always hunting for new scenes to work on in acting class. A director who runs a class may very well be sufficiently taken with an excerpt to want to read the whole thing. (This is how Richard Dreyfuss came to direct one of my plays in Los Angeles.)

The fact is, *anyone* who works in the theater may act as a de facto agent for you. If a designer likes your work, he or she may well drop a word into the ear of a friendly artistic director. My first production in Chicago came about because Joyce Sloane, a friend who was one of Second City's producers, was also on the board of half the theaters in town. As a result of her casual phone call to the Victory Gardens Theater, I ended up doing one play a year with that company for five years.

There are any number of ways to become a part of the theater community. Many theaters are more than delighted to accept volunteer help. A small company is more likely to be interested in reading your script if, say, you've pitched in to get out a mailing. Many theaters also offer classes taught by members of the staff. If you live in the New York area, a visit to Ensemble Studio Theater's summer conference, for instance, will certainly lead to making contact with committed theater professionals. Attend readings at New Dramatists and other developmental companies. If you don't live near New York, make it your business to research where in your area new plays are produced and/or given readings. Go to a local bar afterwards and discuss the work. During the course of the conversation, you may well encounter someone who is simpatico and a potential collaborator.

If you don't live in or near a metropolitan area, you may find this more difficult. Because theater requires access to a large-enough population base to draw sufficient audience to fill the seats of a play's run, by definition the theater is mostly an urban phenomenon.

A piece of advice relating to breaking into TV and films: One-acts make great introductions. Scouts for producers and studios tend to descend on one-act festivals; in one evening they get to see what a handful of writers are capable of doing in a short form. The immediate result of the production of the first, sixty-five-minute version of *The Values of Names* was a contract to develop a situation comedy for Embassy Television. I was hired to adapt *Pack of Lies* for TV because its director, Antony Page, saw, liked, and remembered the production at Lincoln Center of my one act, *Stops Along the Way*. A short play called *Routed*, which was given at the Victory Gardens Theater and Ensemble Studio Theater, attracted the attention of a director named David Ullendorff, who made it into a short film that picked up a number of awards, was run on the Arts & Entertainment Channel and Showtime, and has led to doors opening for other film commissions.

I'm not saying that networking (awful word) alone will put you over the top. Obviously, you have to respond to an opportunity with writing good enough that the people you meet will want to pursue it. But you can certainly put yourself into circumstances that will make it more likely others will give you that opportunity.

Perhaps the single most important professional step you can make as a playwright is to join the Dramatists Guild.

In *Long Day's Journey into Night*, Eugene O'Neill has the character based on his father, actor-manager James O'Neill, refer to "that God-damned play I bought for a song." In fact, this is how it used to be—playwrights commonly sold their work outright to producers. A play could run for years—on Broadway and then on tour—and make fortunes for its star and impresario while its author could die penniless.

Then someone proposed a radical idea: Instead of selling scripts, playwrights would retain ownership and *lease* performance rights to producers in return for royalties based on the productions' gross receipts. The producers of the time, of course, resisted the idea of an arrangement by which they would have to share what they saw as their income. In order to bring pressure to bear, the better-known playwrights banded together and refused to allow productions of their works until the producers agreed to recognize a minimum basic contract that established rights, percentages, and procedures for Broadway and other first-class productions. The producers thought they would be able to fill the gap by importing British plays instead. Our British brothers and sisters demonstrated their solidarity by refusing to be a party to this. They withheld their work, and finally the producers relented and accepted the principle of a standardized first-class contract. Ever since 1920 the Dramatists Guild has safeguarded this contract and monitored the productions of members.

This makes the Dramatists Guild sound like a union, but, for subtle legal reasons, technically it isn't one. (Unions are entities designed to help employees deal with management. Not being employees, dramatists cannot unionize.) Think of it instead as a kind of trade organization through which common concerns are addressed.

What sort of common concerns?

These days, few plays originate in the Broadway economy; most begin their lives in nonprofit venues. (It tells you something about how the business has changed when artists such as Stephen Sondheim and Neil Simon, who established their reputations in the commercial world, now develop their material at South Coast Rep and Playwrights Horizons.) The minimum basic first-class contract for a Broadway production may come too late to protect the writer's interest if he or she has been compelled in a prior, noncommercial production to give up key artistic rights and knuckle under to financial demands.

I know of one playwright who, in order to secure a second stage production at a theater in Chicago, signed over to that theater forty percent of the film rights! A film is indeed going to be made, and that theater is going to realize a good deal more than the relatively small amount it took to mount that modest production. I can see some justification in the theater having some participation, but forty percent for a regional, second-stage premiere is excessive. But the playwright felt that if he wanted the theater to go ahead with the production, he had no choice in the matter. So he capitulated.

It was to provide protection to members against this kind of extortion that the Dramatists Guild decided to look into the possibility of some kind of standardized contract to deal with plays premiered in companies associated with the League of Regional Theaters. The Guild's initial impulse was to negotiate a contract with League representatives. The League declined to negotiate. So, after researching the kinds of contracts Guild members had received from League theaters in the past and factoring in what the membership considers to be basic rights, the Guild issued a proposed contract.

The LORT companies didn't take kindly to it. They maintained that because playwrights (unlike actors, directors, designers, and so on) are not technically employees, we have no right to a standardized agreement. Guild members responded that though we are not employed by the theaters, the producing organizations are still at an overwhelming advantage when negotiating terms with most of us. Unless you're a writer with the profile of a David Mamet, Wendy Wasserstein, or Stephen Sondheim, it's hard to bring much muscle to bear when dealing with what are very often large institutions with multimillion-dollar budgets. More often than not, we are offered contracts with a take-it-or-leave-it attitude. Of course, we writers want to see our stuff done, so is it any surprise that mostly we've choked back our irritation and taken it?

Initially, the LORT companies responded to the Guild-endorsed contract by ignoring it, insisting on continuing their practice of negotiating with writers on a case-by-case basis. By and large, the Guild membership, including its best-known writers, responded as our forebears did: They announced their commitment to refuse the production of any of their scripts—new or old—under any contracts not substantially consistent with the Guild contract. The hope was that having nothing contemporary to produce, either separately or in concert the members of LORT would have to enter into a dialogue with the organization most professional dramatists have chosen to represent our interests. At this writing, the battle continues, but a long list of major, LORT-affiliated theaters either have made the commitment to use the Guild contract or have come up with contracts consistent with Guild-endorsed principles. Ultimately, I am confident that these principles will indeed be accepted by most, if not all, of the LORT companies.

The central issue in this battle is respect. A theater that tells dramatists that it doesn't want to grant us the right, for instance, to participate meaningfully in casting the premieres of our work is sending a message that it doesn't believe we are to be trusted with serious responsibility. The producers grudgingly concede we are usually necessary because we supply the text, but they would as soon grant us power in production as they would give an eleven-year-old the keys to a Mercedes. For too many years, playwrights accepted this de facto assumption of infantilism. Rightly, the membership decided it was time for a change. The battle for fair, standardized contracts with producers is not over arcane fine print. It is about artists claiming their just due: the full rights and responsibilities of artistic adulthood. If we were smart and perceptive enough to create scripts worth producing, odds are we are smart and perceptive enough to collaborate substantively in their production.

Whether or not you are a Guild member, the staff stands ready to assist you if you have questions about how this issue may relate to your particular circumstance. The address: The Dramatists Guild, 234 W. 44th St., New York, New York 10036. The phone number: 212–398–9366.

I see another area of friction growing between dramatists and resident theaters over the development of new work:

Movies and television have long been an influence on the stage. Not just subject matter—for example, shows about Hollywood like *City of Angels*, *Speed-the-Plow* and *Hurlyburly*—but also the adaptation to the stage of cinematic devices such as optical wipes, flashbacks, and so forth. But the influence is beginning to extend beyond subject matter and technique. Increasingly, I find my dealings with nonprofit theaters are echoing patterns familiar from dealings with film and TV companies.

The developmental process has become disturbingly similar to Hollywood development, with the writer often being ordered to satisfy the complaints of test audiences at readings or to accommodate the producers. (The nadir for me came when a nonprofit producer asked me to rewrite a script to conform to his political sympathies! When I told him I didn't think it was my job to articulate *his* values, he canceled the production.) And now I hear about theaters where writers are expected to "pitch" projects, much as one does when trying to get film and TV assignments. And, as also happens in Hollywood offices, the artistic directors and literary managers think it appropriate to amend the stories in the meeting, the clear message being that if you want the commission, you'd better embrace their suggestions. In the process, however, much of what is individual about the dramatists' voices and visions gets lost, homogenized.

This similarity in the behavior of the nonprofits and the studios may be the product of their organizational similarities. The studios have to crank out a certain amount of product in order to stay in business. They have been headed by some of the highest-paid people in film and TV—Guber and Peters, Katzenberg and Eisner, Sherry Lansing, and so forth—to keep the machinery running.

Similarly, the nonprofit theaters usually have subscription seasons to fill. And they, too, are headed by the highest-paid people in their arena—more artistic directors make in excess of $50,000 a year out of the nonprofits than do playwrights. In fact, some artistic directors make substantially in excess of $100,000 a year. Need I say that not many dramatists—in the commercial arena, much less the noncommercial—do that well, year in, year out?

It is sad but demonstrably true that even in the arts, the amount of respect one is given corresponds to the amount of money one is paid. This financial imbalance in the relationship between the nonprofit producers and dramatists has gone a long way to reversing what I believe to be their proper roles. A significant number of artistic directors apparently view them-selves in much the same way the studio heads view themselves. They have become the ruling class of the theater, and drama-tists are there to serve the glory of their administration. In film and TV, writers are hired by the studios to work *for* them. Con-tractually, as I've mentioned, dramatists are not hired by the-aters; they lease to the companies the right to stage their scripts. In actuality, however, I have witnessed dramatists increasingly being treated as employees, subject to direct orders and oleaginous paternalism.

With the death of the commercial marketplace as the major generator of new material, this development is in some ways a historical inevitability.

But here is my concern: If there is less and less difference in the way writers are treated in Hollywood as opposed to the way they're treated in the nonprofits, then there will be less and less reason for writers to write plays. If dramatists are handled by the nonprofits in the same casually condescending manner that is standard operating procedure at many of the studios, they're going to prefer the consolation of studio wages.

And the talent drain will accelerate and the theater will suffer for it.

17

CHAPTER

Parting Words

SOME YEARS AGO, I WAS INVOLVED IN CASTING A COMPANY FOR an off-Broadway revue. The intention was to get together a group of actors with whom I would collaborate on a collection of satiric scenes. They would improvise, I would then write material based on the best of the improvs, and finally, in rehearsal, we would polish these pieces together. Well, that was the *intention*.

The director and I decided we would interview anybody who wanted to be considered. After all, if you're going into a project on the understanding that the material will be drawn out of the experiences, priorities, and imaginations of the cast, it's important that the actors you decide to work with have something interesting to draw upon. So we came up with a few questions to get an idea of what was on their minds. One of the key questions was, "What do you read?"

More often than not, the answer was "the trades" and books on show business. When pressed, most of them said they spent very little time looking at hard news or editorials in the papers. (One actor said he had given up reading newspapers because they only bummed him out.) So what we encountered, by and large, was a group of actors eager to satirize a society about which they had little or no knowledge.

Well, we finally managed to put together a cast. They were talented and smart people, but, in common with most of the others who auditioned, their knowledge was mostly about show biz. So, we ended up with a daring satirical revue with several sketches about actors and auditions and, well, you get the idea.

This was in 1977. I doubt that I would find it much different were I to run similar auditions today. Show people's obsession with show business seems to be stronger than ever.

In the 1991–92 season, with the exception of *Falsettos*, every single musical that premiered on Broadway and most of the ones off-Broadway either told stories that touched on show business or were conceived as parodies of show-biz conventions. *Nick and Nora* was set in Hollywood; *Crazy for You* was about putting on a show; the kids in *Metro* had a similar desire; *Jelly's Last Jam* was a biography of jazz pianist Jelly Roll Morton; *Ruthless*, a marriage between *The Bad Seed* and *All About Eve*, concerned a monstrous little girl who killed in order to get a part in a school play; *Return to the Forbidden Planet* was a take-off on an old science-fiction movie; the title character in *Eating Raoul* was an aspiring performer, and so on and monotonously so forth. This is not my idea of a healthy situation.

I'm not saying that all of these projects are lousy. I like a lot of the shows I've listed. And I can't deny that a couple of my own plays draw on theatrical backgrounds.

But maybe it's time to remember that part of the theater artist's mandate is to reflect the concerns of the larger world in which we live—a world that includes a good deal more than dressing rooms, rehearsal halls, theater, and the media. Hard as it may be for some in the theater to believe, there are people for whom the rigors of show business are not of paramount importance. There are political and social issues that cry out for dramatic treatment. There are huge and fascinating chapters in our history that would make thrilling theater. A world so filled with ideas and conflict should stimulate its artists to spend more time exploring matters of greater importance than whether yet another struggling actor or singer or writer or director or dancer or whatever is going to make the big time.

After all, the roots of the theater are in the urge to deal with the spiritual and social issues of the day in a public arena. Before Gutenberg, the theater was about the massest medium there was. In ancient Greece, you'd get thousands of people into an amphitheater and put on plays that wrestled with the large questions: What was one's relationship to the gods, to the state, to other states, to one's neighbor?

Shakespeare, of course, also wrestled with these questions. The history cycle from *Richard* II to *Richard* III deals with the issue of what qualities are required to be a good monarch, an issue of vital concern to an audience that knew all too well that the character of a king or queen could translate into misery or glory for the subjects.

The point I'm trying to make is that theater artists of the past regarded themselves as citizens—members of the same world as the people who came to see them. Their social status might have been different from their audience (once upon a time an actor couldn't stay in certain hotels much less be elected President), but they recognized and dealt with common concerns.

Lately, though, I believe actors, writers, and directors have increasingly put distance between themselves and their fellow citizens. Some of this has to do with the state of arts training. When you go to an acting school, for instance, the curriculum generally includes speech, scene analysis, fencing, and a lot of other useful craft studies. But there are few drama schools that require more than a token look at other disciplines. Is it any wonder that these young actors emerge waving professional degrees, eager to begin careers but ill equipped to represent any wider experience than that of life in the theater? And since, as I said at the beginning of this book, our playwrights frequently begin as actors, they too tend to know little of the world beyond their immediate interest and experience—show business.

The best theater has not been separate from the society of which it is a part. Most of the glorious moments of the American stage can be traced to some degree of social awareness.

Eugene O'Neill came out of a politically committed group of people. Lillian Hellman's plays consistently focused on the impact of society on individuals. Clifford Odets was the product and a leading voice of the left-leaning Group Theater, members of which subsequently went on to found the Actors Studio, which provided Tennessee Williams, Arthur Miller, and William

Inge with the artists to interpret their works. Second City began as the response of a number of well-read, ferociously intellectual alumni of the University of Chicago (a university, by the way, that offered no theatrical training) to what they saw as the stultification and moral hypocrisy of the 1950s. David Mamet and David Rabe found the inspiration for their writing in the search for values in the wake of Vietnam and Watergate.

In other words, most of the greatest achievements have been the product of artists who were deeply involved in the passions of their times.

This is not to say I'm calling for our actors, writers, and directors to bend their art to propagandistic purposes. But I think we would have a far healthier theater if more knew something about history, philosophy, psychology, and the social sciences. As art is inevitably a product of the artist's experience, we're more likely to enjoy a broader range of dramatic subjects if our artists have more experience in the world outside show business.

All of which leads me to express the hope that you will look at the editorial page of the paper as well as the entertainment section. That you will make an effort to cultivate friends outside of the theater if just to remind yourself that there are such people and that their problems and concerns have just as much right to be presented in dramatic form as do those of the artist.

Earlier in this book, I urged writers to do some reading in the field of ethics. I also hope that you will sample other branches of philosophy as well as psychology, sociology, and anthropology—disciplines that deal with both the ideal and the reality of human behavior. As I have insisted throughout these pages, the portrayal of human behavior is the dramatist's stock-in-trade. The more tools you have to analyze it, the better you'll understand it and the more that understanding will inform and enrich your work.